D1354892

21126

(1986)

£4

TRW

ENTERPRISE
to
ENDEAVOUR

Yankee. After *Whirlwind* she was the largest of the 1930 Js and the only one to keep racing until 1937.

Britannia, 1924, before being
altered to bermudan rig.
/ *Beken*

ENTERPRISE to ENDEAVOUR

The J-Class Yachts

NEW UPDATED EDITION

IAN DEAR

Editors Inc

London

First published 1977
New updated edition 1986

ISBN 0 946052 04 2

All rights reserved. No part of this
book may be reproduced or transmitted
in any form or by any means, electronic
or mechanical, including photo-copying,
recording or by any information storage
and retrieval system, without permission
from the Publisher in writing.

Design by Anthony Wirkus

© Ian Dear, 1977, 1986

Published by Editors Ink,
4 Kings Road, London SW19
Printed by Ian Allan Printing Ltd,
Addlestone, Surrey

"Rainbow"

Contents

The publishers would like to acknowledge
Champagne Mumm, sponsors of the Admiral's Cup
and the WORC, for their support in the publication
of this title.

To all my family, both large
and small, but especially to
Wendy.

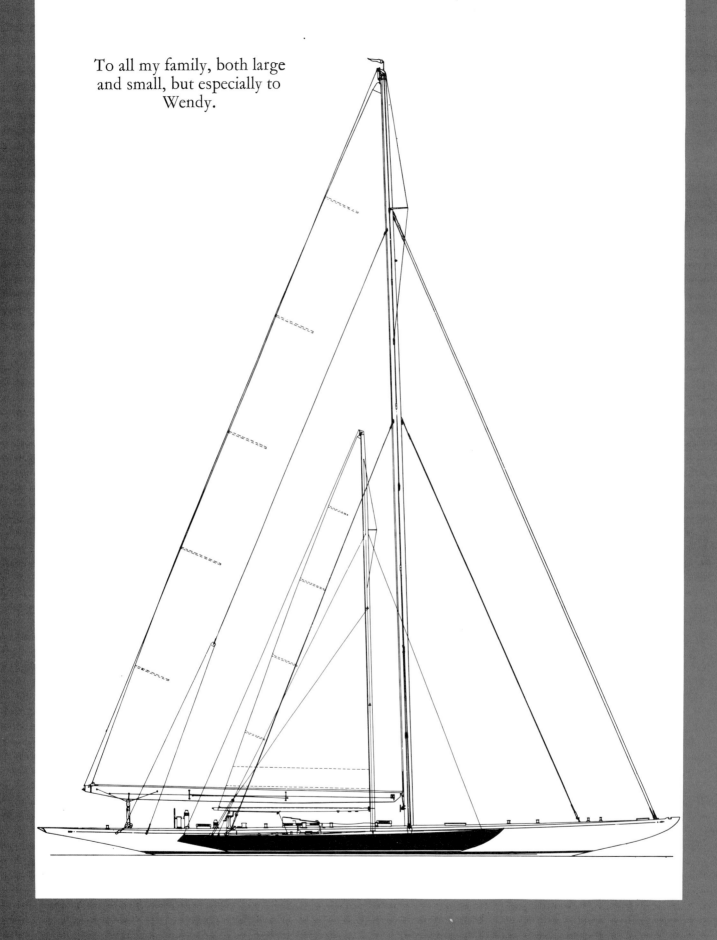

Foreword
Olin J. Stephens II

The opportunity to read in manuscript Ian Dear's story of the J's has brought back some very happy memories. It is especially fun to recall the people and the boats. In July 1931, just before Cowes Week, we sailed *Dorade* up from Plymouth where we anchored off Cowes in the early morning darkness. We came on deck after daybreak to find ourselves almost alongside the King's yacht, *Britannia*. I had not imagined that a yacht could be so beautiful. Our crew were later received on board the Royal Yacht, *Victoria and Albert*, by her owner, King George V, an experience we all remember and appreciate to this day. Later we saw the big class, including the Js, racing in the Solent and, even now, no reminders are necessary to picture *Britannia* and *Westward* with their huge rigs. *Britannia* would then have been in her thirty-eighth year.

G.L. Watson, *Britannia*'s designer, regretfully was before my time but I met two of my heroes, William Fife later, and that summer in England, Charles Nicholson. Of the older generation in America, I knew Nathanial Herreshoff and was fortunate to be able to sail with Clinton Crane on *Weetamoe* in 1934.

Charles Nicholson was very kind and helpful to me when I returned to England in 1932 as a member of the American Six Metre Team. His example of openness and friendship with younger colleagues has offered an example which is not always easy to follow when they are successful in competition.

Clinton Crane was particularly good to me. He had studied naval architecture and designed many yachts as a younger man, but later became head of a big industrial firm and continued to design yachts for himself and his friends as a hobby. In the late twenties, his successes in the 6-Metre Class brought several prospective owners to him and he steered them toward me, wishing I think to encourage a younger man and also preferring not to take work away from a professional.

The new 'Sixes' came out in 1930, the same year that Mr. Crane had done *Weetamoe*, the fastest J of that year. Her story is told in the pages that follow.

Before the 1934 season, *Weetamoe* had been bought by Frederick Prince who invited Mr Crane on board for the America's Cup trials of that year. It was through Mr Crane that I, too, became a member of her afterguard. From a racing point of view, the summer was not a success, but I had a wonderful chance to take part in big boat sailing and to become initiated into both the design and organisational problems of J Class sailing.

During the summer of 1936 my brother Rod had a similar opportunity when Harold Vanderbilt invited him on board *Rainbow* where he became familiar with the rig and many structural details which have always been his special interest. I am sure it was his effectiveness on *Rainbow* that led Mr Vanderbilt to invite us to collaborate with Starling Burgess in 1936 when he decided to go on with a new J-boat to be called *Ranger*.

The J-Class recalls an era of successful international racing. The world of yachting is but one example of constancy and change and today's efforts to make international racing work on a world-wide basis contain elements of both the old and the new. The author's description of how it all worked in the thirties will offer guidance and encouragement to those of us working on the problems of today.

Left: A modern 12-metre, *Columbia*, superimposed on *Ranger*, the Super J./*Stephens*

7

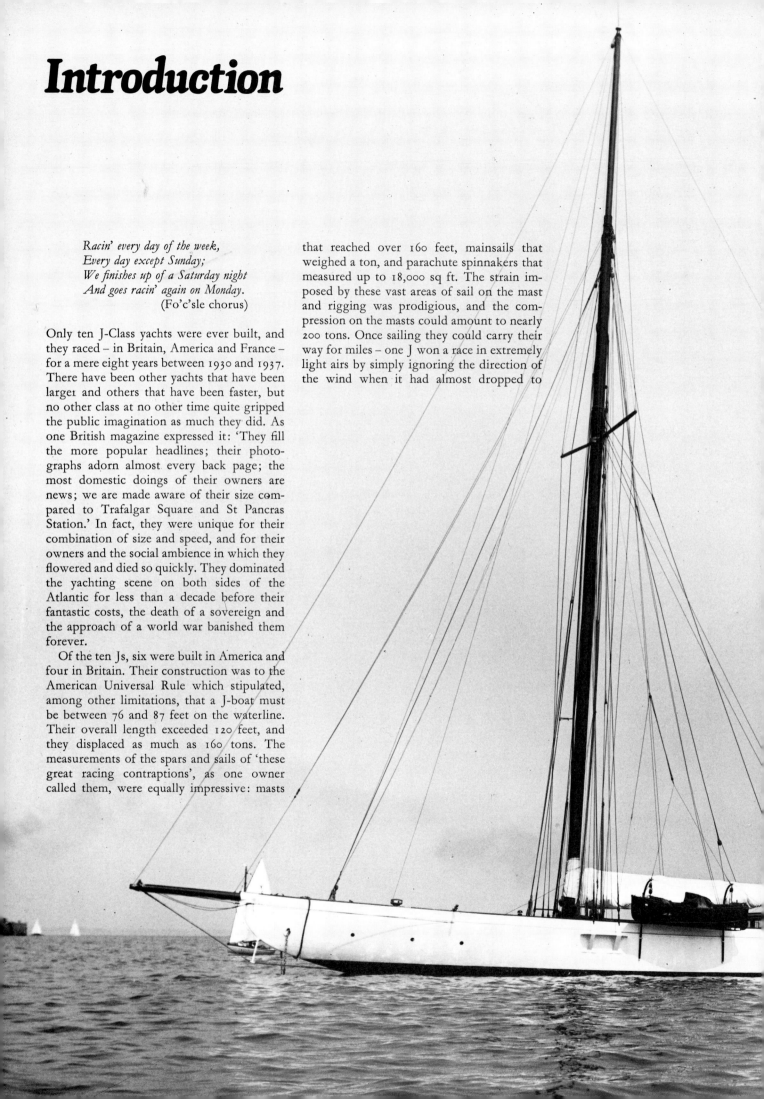

Introduction

Racin' every day of the week,
Every day except Sunday;
We finishes up of a Saturday night
And goes racin' again on Monday.

(Fo'c'sle chorus)

Only ten J-Class yachts were ever built, and they raced – in Britain, America and France – for a mere eight years between 1930 and 1937. There have been other yachts that have been larger and others that have been faster, but no other class at no other time quite gripped the public imagination as much they did. As one British magazine expressed it: 'They fill the more popular headlines; their photographs adorn almost every back page; the most domestic doings of their owners are news; we are made aware of their size compared to Trafalgar Square and St Pancras Station.' In fact, they were unique for their combination of size and speed, and for their owners and the social ambience in which they flowered and died so quickly. They dominated the yachting scene on both sides of the Atlantic for less than a decade before their fantastic costs, the death of a sovereign and the approach of a world war banished them forever.

Of the ten Js, six were built in America and four in Britain. Their construction was to the American Universal Rule which stipulated, among other limitations, that a J-boat must be between 76 and 87 feet on the waterline. Their overall length exceeded 120 feet, and they displaced as much as 160 tons. The measurements of the spars and sails of 'these great racing contraptions', as one owner called them, were equally impressive: masts that reached over 160 feet, mainsails that weighed a ton, and parachute spinnakers that measured up to 18,000 sq ft. The strain imposed by these vast areas of sail on the mast and rigging was prodigious, and the compression on the masts could amount to nearly 200 tons. Once sailing they could carry their way for miles – one J won a race in extremely light airs by simply ignoring the direction of the wind when it had almost dropped to nothing and heading straight for the line – and they could take up to five minutes to tack and regain their speed. Steering a J was an exhilarating experience. As one helmsman wrote, 'Racing a J-boat in a moderate wind is like playing a violin. She is very sensitive to the touch of your hand on the wheel. In many cases the skipper sits on the deck, to leeward of the wheel, steering by a thumb and a finger, getting the feel, watching the luff of the sail or any other sign that will guide him. But in a breeze, particularly running down wind, she is a wild beast sometimes, and it takes strength to steer her.' He was certainly right about that. One J-boat threw her helmsman clear over the steering wheel.

And it was not only the measurement figures that were large: the sums of money involved were huge, too. It has been reckoned that the 1930 defender of the America's Cup, *Enterprise*, cost around one million dollars. The British Js were mostly built of steel, but the American Js were nearly all of tobin bronze, an enormously expensive metal, and their designers used the most modern aeronautical engineering techniques and materials regardless of cost.

Four American Js were built in 1930 for the America's Cup challenge of that year: *Enterprise* (80 feet on the waterline), *Weetamoe* (83 feet), *Whirlwind* (86 feet) and *Yankee* (84 feet). The British built only one, *Shamrock V* (81.1 feet), then two years later they built another, *Velsheda* (83 feet). For the 1934 challenge both countries built one J each: *Rainbow* (82 feet) in America and *Endeavour* (83.3 feet) in Britain. And they did the same in 1937, building *Ranger* (87 feet) in America and *Endeavour II* (87 feet) in Britain.

To call any yacht other than these a J is a misnomer but in Britain the Js raced with the 'Big Class' which, before 1930, had consisted of yachts which had been built to another rule, the International, or to none at all. These yachts formed a class of their own when racing and were commonly called, simply, the 'Big Boats', and when the Js came into existence those which survived into the 1930s were, with the exception of *Westward*, altered so that they could rate in the J class. To call them J-boats is wrong but their story is so much a part of the development and history of the Js – and of a great yachting era – that I have covered them in this book. The classification is further confused by the fact that although the 'Big Boats' built before 1930 were not Js, the Js were also called 'Big Boats' when they all started racing together from 1930 onwards.

In America only two yachts were altered to rate in the J-class, *Vanitie** and *Resolute*, but in Britain there were several more: *White Heather II*, *Britannia*, *Astra* and *Candida*. Lovely names, lovely yachts. In America the sailing lives of the Js were usually brief, for they were brought into being for one reason only: to defend the America's Cup. Though *Weetamoe* kept racing in the New York and Eastern Yacht Club cruises between the two challenges of 1930 and 1934 – and took part in the 1934 Trials to choose a defender – the other three built in 1930 were laid up during these years, and *Enterprise* and *Whirlwind* never sailed again.

In Britain the Js became involved in a different tradition: handicap racing in the regattas which took place round the coast during the summer months. In these regattas yachts built to the International Rule raced against one another; and other 'Big Boats', built to no particular rule, could join in too. One of these was the Royal yacht, *Britannia*, and it is with her – and the yachts which raced against her in the late twenties – that the story of the Js really begins.

*Strictly speaking *Vanitie* rated at the bottom of the I-class

Pride of the Ocean

Britannia the pride of the Ocean,
Beloved by the brave and the free.
The shrine of a sailor's devotion
What ship can compare unto thee?

Britannia was built in 1893 and immediately became a subject of the public adulation which continued throughout her life. Several books were written about her, most of them rather full of sentimental thoughts about the 'Sailor King', the past glories of the British Empire, and the great British sporting tradition. Buried beneath this chauvinism, however, is the remarkable story of a truly outstanding racing yacht. Without *Britannia* and the royal interest in yachting there would have been no 'Big Class', and therefore no yachts like *Lulworth* (ex *Terpsichore*), *White Heather* and the 23-Metre *Shamrock*, with which to establish the British regatta circuit again after the First World War. And because, as we have already seen, the Js evolved from the 'Big Class', there would have been no Js to grace the waters on both sides of the Atlantic.

Britannia was designed by G.L. Watson and built at Henderson's Yard on the Clyde. She immediately proved herself a success, becoming the champion yacht in her first year. Seven yachts competed against her that season, and *Britannia* won twenty races to *Valkyrie's* eleven and *Satanita's* seven. The others only won two apiece, except the German Kaiser's *Meteor* which won only one. Perhaps the results did not reflect exactly the relative merits of the yachts, as *Valkyrie* raced only twenty-four times against Britannia's thirty-eight, but the Royal Yacht's record was sufficiently convincing to leave a lasting impression on the contemporary yachting scene.

In the history of yachting, 1893 could certainly be called a vintage year. Across the water, the Americans built no less than five first class cutters – *Navahoe, Vigilant, Colonia, Jubilee* and *Pilgrim* – while in Britain, *Britannia* was joined by *Valkyrie II, Satanita,* and *Calluna. Navahoe*, having crossed the Atlantic at the beginning of the season, competed in many of the races. *Britannia* beat *Navahoe* in four out of their five meetings though losing the Brenton Reef Cup to her in a controversial decision. It was also in 1893 that Lord Dunraven challenged for the America's Cup with *Valkyrie II*. The Americans chose *Vigilant* from the newly built cutters to defend the Cup, and this she successfully accomplished. Two years later, after a row which caused reverberations forty years on, Dunraven again failed to take the Cup back to Britain.

In 1894 *Vigilant* crossed the Atlantic to take part in the English, Irish and Scottish regattas. Her first race against *Britannia* was on the Clyde and organised by the Mudhook Club, which meant all entries had to be helmed by an amateur. *Britannia* won the race after an appalling accident in which *Satanita* ran down and sank the unsuccessful America's Cup challenger, *Valkyrie II*, being steered by Lord Dunraven himself.

At the time yachts of this size were, of course, exclusively manned by professional crews and owners employed professional skippers to steer them. It was generally thought that amateurs were not competent to steer such large vessels, and the *Satanita* incident seemed to enforce the argument against allowing amateurs to take the helm. It is an enduring argument for there are men still alive in Britain today, both amateurs and professionals, who raced in the Js in the thirties who have little respect for each other. The professionals believe the amateurs were just that – part-time dabblers whose knowledge of the sea and the ways of a large yacht was founded on privilege and not on the inherent understanding that comes from belonging to a long line of fishermen born and bred to the sea. On the other hand the amateur regarded the professional of those days as a menial who simply earned his money from labour on yachts and consequently could not act on his own initiative. He was there just to do what he was told. However good he was – and the crews of the Js were undoubtedly very good indeed – he was still just a paid hand. These opposing attitudes are deeply engrained. They evolved from the deeply engrained class differences of British Society, the gentlemen and players

Left: White Heather II before her conversion to J-Class rating./Lay

Above: The early days: the 23-metre *Shamrock* leads *White Heather II* and *Britannia* during Cowes Week, 1928./*The Field*

success): 'And wouldn't that be the *White Heather* just astern of her, Brown?'

Brown: 'Yes, Sir Walter.'

The owner (now completely carried away by success and becoming jocular): 'But, damned if I can recognise the white cutter, which is she, Brown?'

Brown, who appears stricken by deafness, remains silent.

The owner: 'Brown, I asked you a question. I asked you the name of the third cutter.'

Brown's face twitches with anguish and he sucks his teeth.

The owner (heartily to me): 'The old boy's getting deaf.' (Raising his voice) 'Brown, who owns the other white cutter?'

Brown (as if in pain): 'You do, Sir Walter.'

Sir Thomas Lipton who, along with Edward VII – old 'Tum-Tum' – and his son George V, certainly did more for British yachting and for a longer period than any other man, hardly knew one end of a yacht from the other. And the man who bought *Terpsichore* in 1924 and renamed her *Lulworth*, a Mr Weld, was hardly an expert either. He would disappear below about half an hour before a race began with a copy of *The Times* under his arm and often would not come on deck again until the race was well under way. 'Hello,' he would say, casually looking round. 'We've started!' His detachment from the excitement of the start was, not surprisingly, the cause of general amazement.

But the 'Big Boats' of the late twenties were not, for the most part, owned by aristocrats. George V could mix exclusively with his most blue-blooded subjects at the races or out game shooting, but when it came to sailing, arguably his favourite sport, he was among less socially exalted individuals. Perhaps that was why he enjoyed it so much. He certainly loved racing against *Westward* which was owned by an ex-stevedore with the reputation of having the foulest mouth afloat. Certainly the 'Sailor King' was a very ordinary, unassuming man, a martinet in many ways, and the opposite of his father, 'Tum-Tum'. Queen Victoria, one feels, would have approved of him. But whether she would have approved of the people her grandson sailed against is quite another matter, for almost without exception she would have labelled them with that ostracising word: tradesmen.

True, Lord Waring, who owned the 23-Metre *White Heather II* at one time, may have been a cut above the rest; and Charles Hatry, who owned *Westward* before T.B.F. Davis, was a financier – but they both went broke, Hatry in dishonest circumstances. Lipton, of course, started life as a grocer's boy before making a fortune out of tea; Davis was a South African stevedore who had originated from the Channel Islands; Hugh Paul, the

attitude which is mercifully now beginning to fade.

The Americans never laboured under such a disadvantage, taking the best from both worlds. A man like Vanderbilt had the initiative, drive and organising capacity of the amateur but his ability and reputation had the solid foundation of utter professional dedication. American yachts were being raced by amateurs while in Britain a mere handful took the helm – Sir William Burton on some of the *Shamrock*s, Jameson and then Hunloke on *Britannia*. The others watched their yachts sailing in much the same way as a racehorse owner watched his favourite filly – at a distance and without any intention of getting aboard. Some owners allegedly did not even know what their yachts looked like, as this incident overheard by Anthony Heckstall-Smith and recorded in his book *Sacred Cowes*, shows.

The owner (pointing to a cutter with a green hull): 'Brown, that's the *Shamrock* over there, isn't it?'

Brown: 'Yes, that's 'er, Sir Walter.'

The owner (a smile of triumph spreading across his face as he takes courage from

Above: Cowes Roads during
Cowes Week in the late
1920s./*Beken*

Left: Westward, taken from
Lulworth, 1930./*Stroud*

owner of *Astra*, was a maltster; both Fairey and Sopwith were aeroplane manufacturers; Stephenson, owner of *Velsheda* – the only British J not specially built to challenge for the America's Cup – was chairman of Woolworth's in Britain; Sir Mortimer Singer, who had *Astra* built for him was, of course, the sewing machine millionaire; Sir Charles Allom was a decorator and Sir Howard Frank an estate agent. The owner of *Cambria*, Sir William Berry, was a newspaper proprietor.

All were not members of the Royal Yacht Squadron either, and most of them would not have been allowed into the Royal Ascot enclosure for many had been divorced or had been involved in some scandal – as an alleged conversation between the yachting journalist, Brooke Heckstall-Smith, and the King reveals. The tale is told by Heckstall-Smith's son Anthony, who prefaces it by saying that all the new class of yachts, including *Britannia*, carried the letter 'J' on their mainsails.

'Why J?', the King asked my father when he came aboard for the first time in the summer of 1931. My father explained to him that the letter denoted the size, or rating, of the class under the Universal Rule.

'It should have been 'A'', the King said with a suspicion of a smile.

'Why, sir?' my father queried.

'"A" for adultery, because, with the exception of old Davis, I'm the only owner in the class who still has his original wife!' the King chuckled.

The story sounds apocryphal, however, for it somehow seems unlikely that the King would ever have joked about anything so serious as divorce to a journalist. Also, Heckstall-Smith's statement that all the yachts had the letter 'J' on their mainsails is not true, as *Britannia* always retained her number, K1. However, as a comment on British society at that time, it certainly makes its point.

As to what exactly constituted suitable qualifications for membership of the Royal Yacht Squadron during that time, this was certainly a puzzle to many a visitor to Cowes. One American woman according to Anthony Heckstall-Smith was particularly baffled when she questioned her host about the owners of some of the yachts anchored in the Roads – and remember this was the time of Prohibition in the United States.

'Who owns that one over there?', she asked.

'Ernest Guinness,' was the reply.

'What, the guy that makes the Guinness?' Her host nodded.

'And that cute little black steam yacht?'

'That belongs to Richard Hennessy.'

'Hennessy's brandy?'

'The same family,' her host replied.

'What about that big white ketch?' she asked, and was told it belonged to a family which made beer.

Top left: King George V and Queen Mary on the Royal Yacht Squadron's landing stage at Cowes in the 1920s. They came every year for Cowes Week, but the Queen never raced./*The Times*

Bottom left: King George V at the wheel of *Britannia* in 1931. This is almost certainly a publicity photograph as during the 1930s he never took the helm during a race./*The Field*

Below: Britannia in a blow, the kind of weather she really liked./*The Field*

The woman was incredulous.

'You say all those guys make hooch and yet they're members of the Yacht Squadron?'

Her host said, yes, that was so.

'No kidding! And they told me this was a high-hat club!'

High-hat or not the Royal Yacht Squadron certainly had its share of eccentrics and its share of squabbles with the plebeian public. Perhaps the most famous was with Rosa Lewis who was known and loved, or hated, by a whole generation of yachtsmen and young men-about-town. Her heyday, the mid-1920s falls outside the scope of this book but there is a story related by an American yachtsman, Jack Parkinson, which is irresistible if only to show what Cowes Week must have been like then. He well remembers how Rosa, who had bought the house next to the Squadron, used to make audibly disparaging remarks about the members from her side of the fence for there was a long-standing feud between herself and the club. However, she was all for young yachtsmen, Americans especially, and young Parkinson was a favourite of hers.

'In those days', Parkinson wrote, 'at Cowes old sailors in nice pulling-boats provided a taxi service to and from the yachts. Outboards were unknown. The dean of them all, Harry Speed, took us over and was of inestimable help with our laundry and groceries. He was usually in a slightly inebriated condition and spent considerable time in *Nicanor*'s cabin drinking beer and polishing his glass eye which he would remove from its socket.

'We decided Rosa Lewis should be invited for a visit aboard so one lovely calm Sunday afternoon Harry Speed rowed her out. There was no Sunday racing then and the various lords and ladies sat about in dignified majesty on the afterdecks of their large yachts. Getting Rosa aboard presented a problem as she had grown stout and wore a long pink gown surmounted by a huge picture hat. It was unanimously decided that the boatswain's chair shackled to the main-halliard was the best way. Three of us tailed on the halliard and she came out of Speed's boat so easily that we kept her going to the masthead and belayed it. The resulting shrieks and profanity brought all the assembled English nobility to their feet with telescopes in hand. Next day representatives from various yacht clubs advised us coldly that such performances were not approved in Cowes on Sunday afternoons . . .'

Queen Mary was probably furious!

Cowes itself during the late twenties and for most of the era of the Js that followed remained curiously unchanged. Reporting Cowes Week in 1931 for *The Field*, a writer

compared the place with how it had been at the beginning of the century: 'The same parties still crowd into the same little houses and fill the same villas; the same wicker chairs are set out on the club lawn and filled with the identical people who have been pillars of the little town for years. Here they greet each other almost like relations; here they are kindly, considerate, almost affectionate, and the outsider feels almost like an intruder upon a family party.

'They all know each other's histories and secrets, and their conversations bristle with little allusions, the unintelligibility of which to an outsider makes a high and inseparable barrier . . .

'In a changing world the great social festival of Cowes Week has changed scarcely at all, but the rig of the yachts lying in the roadstead would seem as strange to someone of the Victorian period as would the dresses of the ladies on the Squadron lawn.

'Bermuda sails have replaced gaff mainsails and diesel engines have ousted steam; berets are worn by the ladies instead of those quaint straw boaters, and skirts no longer sweep the ground. Nevertheless the Big Class sails the same course as the great cutters did in those gay years at the close of the nineteenth century, while the talk and gossip ashore and afloat remains as unintelligible as ever to the outsider.'

And again, the following year the same paper commented: 'In a changing world Cowes and Cowes Regatta have changed astonishingly little . . . The Royal yacht is at her mooring, her owner is afloat aboard his racing cutter enjoying his favourite sport – racing against other tall-sparred cutters, most evenly matched. Further off lies HMS *Malaya*, the guardship, her grey sides newly painted, her brass work gleaming in the sunlight. There are sighs ashore that this year for reasons of economy *Malaya* will not give the customary ball. This fact and a slight reduction in the number of yachts anchored in the roads are the only indications of the financial problems that confront the world.'

But, as the paper pointed out, even if the people and the ambience hadn't changed, the yachts had. In fact, during her long career *Britannia* had no less than seven rigs (see fig 1) and from them it is interesting to note that the progression towards a taller, narrower sailplan was a steady one, and that the jump from gaff to bermudan rigging did not take place in one bound. The development from the triple-headed rig of jib topsail, jib, and staysail, to the double-headed and then single-headed came well after the introduction of bermudan rigging on the marconi mast.

From 1900 to 1920 *Britannia* was rigged for cruising and the alterations made for the 1926 racing season were short-lived as they proved unsatisfactory. The 1931 rig was to adapt her to the Universal Rule for Js, and her final rig in 1935 was to change her from a triple-headed to a double-headed rig with the famous Park Avenue boom, of which more later.

As we have seen, *Britannia* from 1913 was sailed by an amateur, Sir Philip Hunloke, who was officially the King's representative on board. He was King George's representative not because the King was the King but simply because every owner in those early days had a representative on board his yacht, and that man was always an amateur. The job of the owner's representative was not onerous: he was always an expert on racing tactics and always a gentleman – the sort who pronounced 'tactics' as 'tatics'. His major job was to sign the declaration after the race that his yacht had conformed to the rules and had sailed the course correctly. This could not be left to the professional skippers as, apparently, they were 'such foul sailors' (as one expert amateur J-Class helmsman described them) they would break every rule in

Above: On the lawns of the Royal Yacht Squadron. This is Cowes Week 1935, but somehow the scene is timeless./*The Field*

Left: Yachting the grand way: This dramatic shot was taken from the foremast of *Westward*. Under the parasol is Lady Albermarle./*Egan*

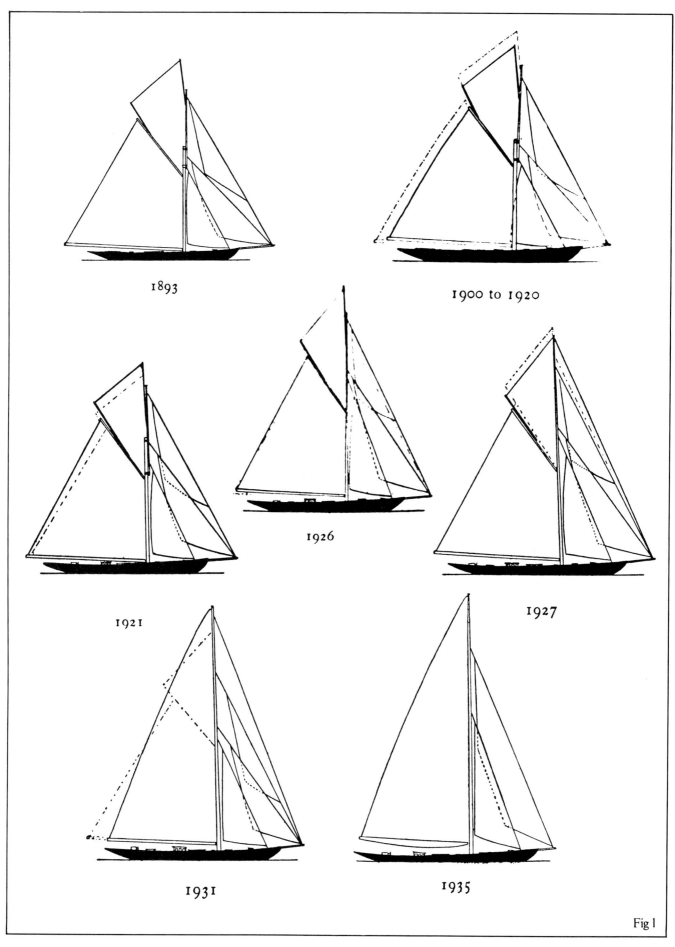

1893

1900 to 1920

1926

1921

1927

1931

1935

Fig 1

the book if they thought they could get away with it. Owner's representatives were, of course, unknown in the United States.

In most ways Hunloke was a typical product of his era: a member of the Royal Yacht Squadron from early youth, imbued with the English upper-class attitude that was reflected in his sailing philosophy. 'I have raced with and against many professionals. Gomez, Ben and Bill Parker, Sycamore, Charles Beavis and Mountifield, were all fine seamen, but I think Sycamore was the cleverest. The common criticism of the professionals was that they would go for some immediate advantage without seeing the race as a whole – as a thing that needed a long view. I believe that the criticism was justified. If they had paused to think they would not so often have luffed a rival off the course at the expense of going off the course themselves . . . I don't suppose for a moment that the professionals would not have admitted this if you had argued it out with them' (obviously, Hunloke never bothered to!) 'but it was surprising how often when the temptation came to score off the nearest opponent they gave way to it, without considering the effect upon the race as a whole. A little imagination was necessary, and there they often failed in spite of their immense experience. I am sure that the amateurs have shown rather more imagination.'

Above: On board *Britannia*: Queen Mary chats with the King's Sailing Master, Sir Philip Hunloke (left), while King George V has a word with Captain Turner./*Turner*

Left: Captain Fred Mountifield, the veteran skipper of *White Heather II*. Later, he was skipper of the J, *Velsheda*./*The Field*

Far left: Britannia had seven different rigs during her long career. They show very well how sail plans changed and developed during her 42 years of racing and cruising./*from* The King's Britannia *by John Irving*

19

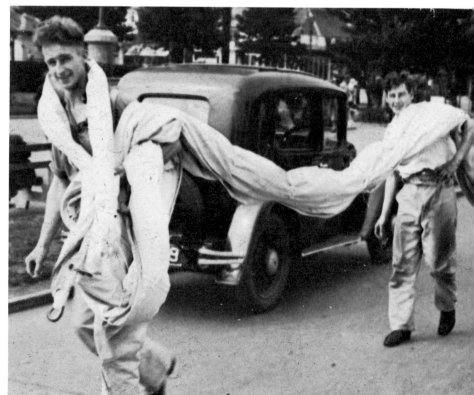

What the professionals thought about Hunloke's tactics is not recorded but it is undeniable that he was a helmsman of great skill and determination. Curiously, Anthony Heckstall-Smith considered Hunloke himself to have very little imagination!

Hunloke also pointed out that he thought the professionals rather too ready to stand on their rights. In other words if they had the right of way they kept their course, or if they thought the rules were on their side they enforced them. A not unreasonable attitude one would have thought. After all, they were racing for prize money in a period when there were no state health services or generous unemployment benefits and their means of livelihood for the winter months – fishing – was notoriously risky. But Hunloke thought this attitude 'did not make for the consideration with which every game ought to be played'!

Certainly, from what the still living crew members of the crews of Big Boats say, *Britannia* was given no quarter – though Jim Thaw, who sailed on several of the Js, says that only *Westward* made *Britannia* tack when the King was on board; the others kept clear

skippers. If they were to win prize money the gear had to be in first-class condition for a yacht was often driven to its limit. Discipline on board was as rigorous as anything aboard a battleship, and the crew was up at five-thirty and had scrubbed the decks and polished the brass long before they had breakfast. In the days of the gaff rig, it took several hours to ready a yacht for a race. And when it was over a cover wasn't just thrown over the mainsail. It was taken off, even if there was a race the next day. The mainsheet was taken off the boom, too, and all ninety fathoms of it was neatly coiled!

The skipper knew his crew well – usually they came from his own home town or village – and they went with him if he changed boats. It was the shipper and his two mates who, with the aid of a local pilot, judged the speed and direction of wind, tide, and rival yachts. Even in the 1930s when the owners steered themselves they usually followed the advice of their skippers. The professional men, in fact, had it very much their own way for many years.

Hunloke, however, raced and commanded *Britannia* himself. When his first post-war skipper, Charlie Leavett, gave orders to douse the spinnaker without reference to Hunloke, Hunloke soon made his feelings known.

'I did not give the order to in spinnaker. Haul the spinnaker out again.'

'In that case I suppose I might as well go down below,' Leavett replied.

Far left top: Working on a J's mainsail at Ratsey and Lapthorn's sail loft at Gosport./*Knight*

Far left bottom: A J's mainsail weighed nearly a ton and it took a team of men to lift one./*Knight*

Left: The headboard of a J's mainsail./*Knight*

Below: Some of *Britannia*'s crew. They served in her year after year under Captain Turner. The bo'sun, Ernie Friend, reading the newspaper, was drowned during a race, one of the few fatal accidents to occur during the 'Big Boat' era./*Turner*

Bottom: Part of the crew of *Shamrock V*. They came from places as far apart as Brixham in Devon and Whitstable in Kent. Several came from the East Coast fishing villages of Wivenhoe, Tollesbury and West Mersea, which provided so many of the crew for the J-Class./*Heard*

even if they had the right of way. The King's yacht she might be, but in a race which meant a pound to each hand for a win, if a rival yacht could cut her out from the start she would. (They rarely did! Hunloke was brilliant at manoeuvring *Britannia* on the start line). To the modern yachtsman this is, of course, the right and proper attitude, but it's easy to see why Hunloke might get annoyed when, with his Sovereign on board, he was luffed off course by a tough, determined East Coast fisherman who seemingly wanted just prize money.

But Hunloke who was kind and courteous as well as fair, gave the professionals unstinting praise where he thought they deserved it. They were, he said, wonderfully quick in picking up a change in weather and 'they would spot a different slant of wind, or a harder wind, perhaps a long way off, which the amateur would not have noticed and they would go well off their course to get the benefit of it . . . Again, the professionals were excellent at caring for a ship and her gear, and especially good at trimming sails.'

The care and maintenance of the yacht was always uppermost in the minds of professional

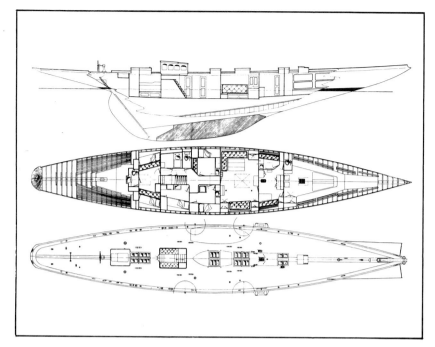

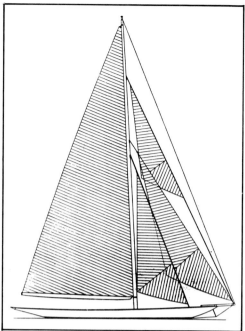

'Yes, by all means,' Hunloke snapped back, 'and stop there.'

This clash did not augur well and it was obvious that *Britannia* could not be raced properly with two such different personalities on board. In 1923 Leavett was replaced by Albert Barr Turner, one of the best known of the East Coast skippers. Turner stayed with *Britannia* to the end. He and Hunloke hit it off straight away and in their first season together the royal yacht won twenty-three flags in twenty-six races, and eleven of these were firsts.

Britannia's main rivals in the early and middle twenties were *White Heather II* (later converted to J-Class rating), *Nyria* (the first yacht ever fitted with a marconi mast and bermudan rigging), Lipton's 23-metre *Shamrock* (not to be confused with any of his Cup challengers which were numbered I to V), and *Westward*. Then in 1928 two new yachts came on the scene. One of them was *Astra*, a superb creation of Charles Nicholson. She was able to rate with the Js and often beat them on handicap though she was a good deal smaller. She was built for Sir Mortimer Singer by Camper and Nicholson's, Sir Mortimer having sold *Lulworth* – Mr Weld having relinquished her for a more comfortable place to read *The Times* – to a Mr Paton. John Nicholson records in his book, *Great Years in Yachting*, that Sir Mortimer suggested to his father that he should build him two yachts, one for light winds and another for heavy weather, and had to be reminded that yachting was not like horse racing!

The second new yacht was *Cambria* and her owner, the newspaper proprietor Sir William Berry (later Lord Camrose), was also

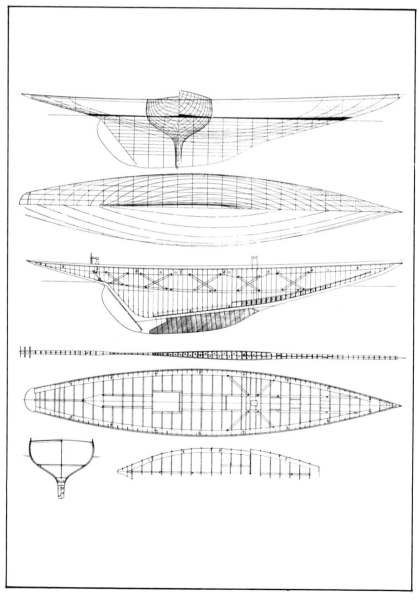

Above: Cambria ready for launching, 1928./*Stroud*

Top far left: The deck and accommodation plan of *Astra*. /*Camper and Nicholson*

Top left: Astra's sail plan. /*Camper and Nicholson*

Left: Astra's lines. Though the smallest yacht to be adapted to the J-Class she won many flags in British regattas. /*Camper and Nicholson*

Top right: Lulworth, taken from aboard *Cambria*, 1928./*Stroud*

Right: Cambria, just after being launched at Fairlie, 1928. /*Stroud*

more of a patron of the sport than a partici-pator. He, according to Pat Egan (one of the most experienced amateurs to race in the Js), thought it might be a good idea to have a second 75-footer. But when he asked his wife if she wanted it, she declined!

Cambria did not have *Astra*'s success. She won her first race at Harwich but hardly gained a flag after that. Albert Stroud, who was racing in her that first year, put it down to the fact that an extra ton and a half of lead was shipped and put aft. 'When we raced the next day the boat was dead. Any-body who knows anything about sailing at all, could feel that the boat was dragging and as sluggish as could be.' But the atmosphere aboard was also bad, as Stroud vividly recalls while recording one of the rare accidents to occur with the Big Boats. '*Astra* was just ahead of us and we were on her weather quarter. Sir William Burton was at the wheel – as always – and I suppose he thought *Astra* was going to luff us so her bore away to go across her stern, but we were just that bit too far ahead and we cut *Astra*'s taffrail completely away, carrying it between our bowsprit and bobstay just like a dog with a bone in its mouth. Of course, that put us out of the race completely and we had to retire. Incidentally, my two brothers, Alf and Harold, were in *Astra* that year, and I heard some of the comments from them. There were strained relations aboard *Cambria* too, Sir William Berry going off very angry indeed, and when I put Mr Fife (*Cambria*'s designer) ashore at Ryde, he remarked to me, "I know what is wrong with the boat", but not en-larging any further than that.' Whatever the cause, *Cambria* only raced for a few seasons and was never converted to rate as a J.

Cambria leading *Candida* during Cowes Week. Note that both yachts are well reefed down./*Beken*

Top: *Cambria*, just before launching./*Stroud*

Above: Until the 1931 season the Big Boats were a mixed bunch. Here the new J-Class yacht, *Shamrock V*, is seen racing against, from left to right, *White Heather II*, *Britannia*, and *Lulworth*, which are still gaff-rigged./*Beken*

Left: Astra with her original sail plan. Later she adopted the double-headed rig./*Camper and Nicholson, Cannes*

Both *Astra* and *Cambria* were built to the new International Rule which came into force in 1928. Although agreement on the new rule between America and Britain only extended to yachts of 14½ metres and under, some encouragement to build the two yachts was at least in part derived from the fact that the rule gave advantage to bermudan rigged boats. But the main encouragement came from two sources. First, the news that a new 21-metre American yacht, *Katoura*, owned by a Mr Tod, had been specially built for racing in British waters and would be crossing the Atlantic for the 1928 season and second, British hopes that the International Rule would be extended to cover yachts of 14½ metres and over. Unfortunately, *Katoura's* visit never materialised and the Americans judged the 1928 International rule to be too restrictive for the bigger yachts. The point was well expressed by Junius Morgan of the New York Yacht Club when he commented: 'We look towards progress in design. The Europeans seem to wish to crystallise design

with a view to retaining the racing life of a boat for the longest period of time.'

So the Americans continued to race their large boats under their own Universal Rule which had been introduced by the great yacht designer Nat Herreshoff in the early 1890s, and adopted by the N.Y.C.C. some dozen years later. In Britain, yachting carried on much as before though a new rule,* a development of one devised in 1920, did restrict the height of sail plans.

It is interesting that Mr Morgan should so clearly show up the fundamental differences of the two countries in their approach to yachting just as international yachting was about to change dramatically. The Americans were accused by their English counterparts of going for perfection by adopting the policy of 'scrap and build'. An English yachting writer wrote: 'I am convinced the Americans are wrong. My reasons go deep, and is fundamental to all things as well as ships. No man, American or any other, can feel full love for anything until time has had her chance to wrap it round his heart. I think it must be agreed that perfection without full love of the thing itself is unattainable. That is fundamental. It is also something of a religious precept; so here I'll say no more.' Which, the modern reader may feel, is just as well.

Sentimental as it is, this passage, when compared with Mr Morgan's statement, really pinpoints one of the reasons why the British effort to wrest the America's Cup had always failed: the will to win was always secondary to the aesthetics and pleasures of playing the game for its own sake. On the other hand, the British have shown how right Morgan was in his judgment of them and still enjoy the fruits of their philosophy. *Shamrock V* is still in commission, *Endeavour* and *Velsheda* are still afloat, and *Astra*, *Cambria* and *Candida* are around too in different parts of the world. In America not one J-boat remains.

Despite the non-appearance of *Katoura* the 1928 season was memorable with the 23-metre *Shamrock* battling it out with the royal cutter – and coming out on top. It was an interesting season, too, for it was the first real clash between the new bermudan rigged yachts, *Astra* and *Cambria*, and the well-proved gaff-rigged boats. Because the modern rig did not come out of the season at all well – the new rule was almost certainly too severe on them – that autumn it was decided that for the following season the bermudan rigged yachts would be allowed an increase of 7.5% in their mast height while the rig allowance for the gaff-rigged vessels was slightly reduced.

*The new formula was rating (metres) =
$$\frac{L + S.A. - F}{2.3}$$

27

Above: Yacht racing in Britain – especially the Big Boats – was very much a spectator sport. Here, on the Green at Cowes, a crowd has gathered waiting for the start of a race./*Beken*

But the bermudan rigged boats proved their superiority in one important aspect: they were simpler. While it took the crew of the gaff riggers literally hours to prepare for a race, with the new rig it took hardly any time at all and fewer men were needed to handle it. *Britannia*'s crew, for instance, was reduced from thirty to twenty-five. When gaff-rigged it had taken her an hour to get under way. With her new rig it took her half that time. Hunloke never looked kindly upon the new Bermudan class. Nor did he like the J class and commented that they were fit only for the Serpentine in a strong breeze. 'Why should anyone in his senses want to put up with all the anxiety you have in the present large bermuda rig yachts in a hard wind? If in a squall one stay goes, or anything goes wrong with the winch, probably everything goes. Some people say that the masts are too high to be stayed properly, and of course there is little enough spread on the deck for staying, but I can't help thinking that the greater part of the trouble is the fashionable tightness of the rigging. The modern winches stretch everything bar tight. Every stay becomes like a violin string. Then if one snaps where are you? In *Britannia* I always used to insist upon the shrouds being kept slightly slack. Then there was some give. The topmast stay

and the preventer backstay are rather a different matter. They can be as tight as you please, because you need absolute fore-and-aft rigidity. But I am sure that the relative slackness of *Britannia*'s shrouds saved us several times when others lost their masts.

'In the race at Babbacombe in 1933 when we had a full sail in a gale I owed much to my fairly slack shrouds and sheets. That makes me think of the difference between English and American waters. What is wrong here in rigging may be right there. The Americans screw everything up as tight as possible, but I fancy, though I have not raced there, that their seas are not the same shape as ours. They have more regular seas, and they have nothing like our tides, which cause short, choppy seas, so their rigging holds well. Here we have to look out for more jerks and jumps, which in my view, are too much for very tight rigging. I believe we have learnt more from the great strength of American rigging than we have learnt from the famous American disciplining of crews and the planning of the afterguard. After all, many of our large yachts have well-trained crews all the members of which have their regular jobs and work in silence.'

It is worth quoting Hunloke at length – and out of sequence as Hunloke was talking

Above: Candida, 1930, under trysail. She was probably making a passage at the time. Taken from *Lulworth./Stroud*

about the Js proper – not only because he was one of the most experienced helmsmen of the time but because he raises questions fundamental to the understanding of what it was like to own and race these huge cutters during the late twenties and early thirties.

Firstly, the new rig saved money. It is surprising that Hunloke did not at least admit that this was an advantage of the bermudan sail. Perhaps in those days gentlemen did not mention money. But it is unlikely that his budget was limitless, for the King could hardly be called a big spender and Queen Mary was notorious for her penny-pinching.*

*When the American yachtsman Gerard Lambert was asked to dinner aboard *Britannia* he was asked whether he'd like a cigar. Lambert said he would – and was offered one which had been cut in half! Another amusing example of the Sovereign's care with money is related by Sir Thomas Sopwith. One year after he'd won the King's Cup his wife visited a West End jeweller who recognised her name. The jeweller told her he'd been asked by Buckingham Palace to send up some samples of gold cups from which the King could choose a suitable one for that year's King's Cup. One was chosen but its lid was returned with the comment that the King could not afford both the cup and the lid!

But, like all the owners of Big Boats, it would have cost him around £2,600 a year to run *Britannia* – and that excluded the making of new canvas which could easily add another £700 a year. During the season a good boat could pick up over £1,000 in prize money, but even so running a Big Boat was not a cheap pastime. So a cut in the wages bill was a welcome saving.

Secondly, while Hunloke expressed very well the anxiety of racing such an enormous vessel in the confined waters of a British regatta course, he did not seem to appreciate that yacht racing in the thirties was a popular sport. The crowds were not only drawn by the beauty of the Js but by the closeness and variety of the racing. In short, the risks were more than offset by the pleasure they gave the public and, in fact, accidents were extremely rare.

Finally, Hunloke mentions the touchy subject of crew and afterguard. When he says the British learnt more about rigging than crew management from the Americans he was, sadly, only too right. His lack of perception on this critical point could be said to be typical of most British owners of that time, though Richard Fairey was possibly an honourable exception. But it proved to be the crucial issue on which the fifteenth, and

closest, challenge for the America's Cup, hinged.

During the winter of 1928/29 Camper and Nicholson's built a new 23-metre, *Candida*, for Mr Herman Andreae, a banker who owned the 19-metre *Corona*, and with her launching the new era of yachting began to be discerned. *Cambria* and *Astra* were modern yachts but their owners and crew were as old-fashioned as the gaff riggers they still raced against. But *Candida* was different, for not only had she a modern rig but also a modern owner. Andreae was not just a patron of the sport; he had raced for years and was an expert helmsman. To ensure that there would be no clash of personalities when he took the helm of his new boat he specifically asked Camper and Nicholson's to provide him with a mate, not a skipper. They put him in contact with Jim Gilbey, who had been Captain Mountifield's mate in *White Heather*. This proved to be a very satisfactory arrangement, and Gilbey emerged as the new type of skipper, who helped and guided the owner, relieved him at the helm when necessary, kept the crew and yacht up to scratch, but who never dictated the tactics when racing, or the running of the yacht generally.

From all accounts Gilbey was a gentle sort of man. 'You know,' he said to yachting journalist John Scott Hughes one evening when they were standing together in the bows of *Candida* at Torquay, 'I don't so much mind

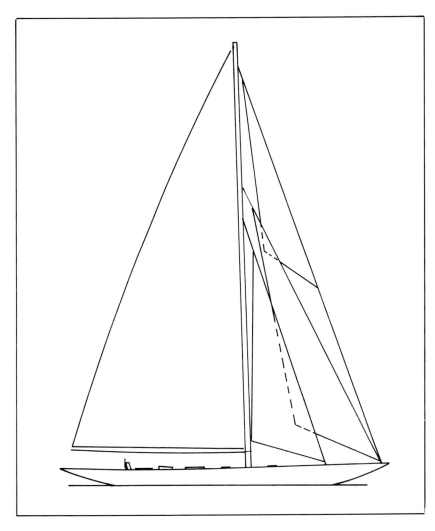

Above: Shamrock V's sail plan.
/Camper and Nicholson

Top left: Herman Andreae at
the wheel of *Candida.* He
belonged to the new breed
of owner./*The Field*

Left: Three hearty cheers now!
It was the custom to cheer the
winner of a race just as owners
always doffed their caps to one
another when passing within
hailing distance./*The Field*

not winning races. All I want is that my
gentleman shall enjoy himself.'

'It was the same dear Gilbey,' Scott Hughes
records when writing about the year the
American J, *Yankee,* raced in British waters,
'who, ordered as the custom is to give the
winner of the race a cheer, mustered his crew
with a quaint command of his own "come on
our side", and, as the yacht approached
Mr Lambert's victorious *Yankee,* in the actual
instant when with cap in hand he was raising
the cheer, scratched his head and turned to the
owner to ask, "What's the name of this 'ere
Yank, Sir?"' '

With three new yachts and three old ones,
the 1929 season promised to be outstanding.
And indeed in many ways it was with the Big
Class making over forty starts. But then the
King became ill and convention dictated that,
with the Sovereign abed, *Britannia* did not
race. Without the King, things could not be
quite the same. Another incident, too,
marred the season. *Astra*'s owner, Sir Mortimer Singer, took his own life and *Astra* was
withdrawn before the Clyde fortnight began.
She had started the season brilliantly with
four wins out of five starts. Singer, like several
of the Big Boat owners, had been involved in

the early aeroplanes. Before the first world
war he had crashed and had been severely
injured. Constant pain had turned him into
an insomniac. *Astra* lay idle for some time
and then was bought by Sir Howard Frank
who sailed her spasmodically the following
summer before Hugh Paul purchased her for
the 1931 season.

Towards the end of 1929 Lipton issued his
fifth and final challenge for the America's
Cup. In the negotiations which always
follow the issuing and acceptance of a
challenge Lipton agreed to build his yacht to
the American Universal Rule, and that the
yacht would be of the J class i.e. between
seventy-five and eighty-seven feet on the
waterline.*

With the American Universal Rule the
'length plus cube root of the sail area' of the
International rule became the 'length multiplied by the cube root of the sail area'. In
other words the tax on sail area was severe,
and, in order to maximise what was allowed,
the higher the aspect ratio the better it was
for driving the hull through the water. Put
simply, under the International Rule an
increase in length meant a corresponding and
appreciable reduction in the sail area while
under the Universal Rule the waterline
could be increased with hardly any penalty
for sail area provided the displacement was
also increased. Under the International Rule
vessels are built that do not differ much in
length, sail area or displacement, while under
the Universal Rule they can vary considerably.

For the design and building of *Shamrock V,*
Lipton went to Camper and Nicholson's.
Shamrock V was the first of his yachts to be
built to Lloyd's A1 scantling requirements,
this stipulation having been agreed between
the Americans and the British earlier to avoid
the construction of lightweight hulls which
in the past had proved both unseaworthy and
expensive.

Of semi-composite construction, *Shamrock
V* had her stem, stern post and counter
timbers of teak and her wooden keel of
English elm. Her lead keel weighed 78 tons.
Her frames were entirely of steel with a
longitudinal 'trough' of steel plates. The
planking was mahogany and the main deck
was laid with yellow pine. The mast, pear-

*'The New York Yacht Club's racing fleet was
classified by letters. For schooners and
ketches there was a first class for yachts over
100 feet, then Class A for yachts between 100
and 88 feet rating, down through classes
B,C,D,E,F,G, and H, the last being yachts not
over 31 feet in rating. Sloops and yawls began
with a first class of over 88 feet rating, and
then were lettered down, I,J,K,L,M,N,P and Q.
the last being yachts rating not over 30 feet but
not less than 25 feet waterline length.'
From *History of the New York Yacht Club*
by John Parkinson Jr.

31

shaped in section, was no less than 162 feet from truck to heel and was constructed of about fifty pieces of silver spruce. *Shamrock V* contrasted strongly with the other British bermudan rigged yachts because, although she carried some 700 sq ft less sail area, her sail plan was 152 feet high compared with the 137 feet of the others.

On the day *Shamrock V* was launched – 14th April 1930 – Lipton's old skipper, Sycamore, was buried. Falling ill during the winter he had retired and Ted Heard had taken his place. Sycamore was one of the great professional skippers, and was obviously greatly loved by the public. 'Old Syc' they called him, or 'Syccy', and knew him to be a man with nerves of steel. Apparently, he had a rather shrill voice which could be heard across the water egging his crew on to greater effort. 'And what are you doing my man?' John Scott Hughes once heard him ask a seaman who was walking away from a half completed task, 'sliding about like a snake in the long grass.' His sarcasm was famous. 'If you gentlemen will come up to windward,' he was once heard to say to some guests on *Shamrock*, 'you will be in the sunshine, altogether more comfortable – *and out of the way of my main boom.*' He was also something of a snob and once, when rebuked for entering an owner's cabin with his cap on, he said, with a twinkle in his eye: 'The fact is I've

Far left: Shamrock V taking part in her first regatta, Harwich, 1930. She appears just to have her nose in front of *Cambria.*/*NYYC*

Left: Ted Heard, *Shamrock V*'s professional skipper./*The Field*

Below: Another view of what is probably the same race at Harwich, but this time *Cambria* is in the lead./*The Field*

been so long with Sir Thomas Lipton I've forgotten what it is to be in the service of a gentleman.'

Apparently, he sometimes got over-excited when racing and was, according to one writer 'difficult to control', which meant, probably, that he broke the racing rules if he thought he had a chance of getting away with it. The 23-metre *Shamrock* was his favourite yacht and he and she and Lipton's representative, Duncan Neill, made an almost unbeatable combination.* 'Burly, sturdy, but straight-backed,' was how John Scott Hughes described him, 'Gold-bearded, boyish-eyed Sycamore when I sailed with him appeared in the prime of life. But he was then 74 years of age.' Sycamore really belongs to a different era to the Js and it was perhaps symbolic that he was buried on the day a new age in British yachting history began.

That first season *Shamrock V* sailed in twenty-two races before departing for

*The 23-metre *Shamrock*'s record was second only to *Britannia*'s. Out of 300 races, she won 190 prizes, 127 first flags. She was broken up at Gourock, Scotland, in 1933.

America, and out of these she won fifteen and came second in four – an outstanding record which had all the contemporary yachting writers speculating wildly on her chances of bringing back the Cup. Special regattas were provided for her, all of which were centred on Cowes, creating what one writer called a 'little season' at the beginning of June. But the truth is that the Yacht Racing Association, the body responsible for alloting handicaps, had expected *Shamrock V* to be beaten boat-for-boat, and so gave her five seconds per mile over a 24-metre. After five races, however, they had to reverse the handicaps and give the other big boats six seconds per mile, but by then *Shamrock V* had several wins already chalked up. Also, she was racing with a hollow spar, no cabin fittings and a centreboard – none of which was allowed at the time. Her rating at the beginning of the season certainly showed how even the experts under-rated the power of the new high aspect sail plan.

By the time she was ready to cross the Atlantic, *Shamrock V* had been raced and tested in races totalling nearly 720 miles, far more than any of her potential adversaries.

No previous challenger had been so well-tuned, none so highly-praised. Why then didn't she win?

The America's Cup races have been analysed and re-analysed in many books, and the 1930 challenge has been discussed at length along with the rest. On the whole it was a dull series for *Shamrock V* did not win a race nor did she look like doing so. It was not so much a case of what went wrong but of just not being nearly good enough. The Americans had the distinct advantage of being able to build four boats – *Enterprise, Weetamoe, Whirlwind* and *Yankee* – to Britain's one, all of them different lengths to seek out the best performances for racing under the Universal Rule. For *Shamrock V*, Nicholson chose 80 feet, a length almost identical to that of *Enterprise* – the eventual defender – though it was later to emerge that in common with other classes, though for different reasons, it was better to build a J to the limit of the class rule.

A comparison of the hull lines of the competing Js does not reveal any weakness in the challenger, but they looked very different indeed. Doubtless Nicholson's

Above: Part of the spectator fleet for the 1930 America's Cup races. Note the hazy conditions./*The Field*

Top left: Shamrock V below looking forward./*Rosenfeld*

Bottom left: Shamrock V, the 1930 challenger, making heavy weather of it during her Atlantic crossing. Taken from Lipton's diesel yacht, *Erin*. / *Heard*

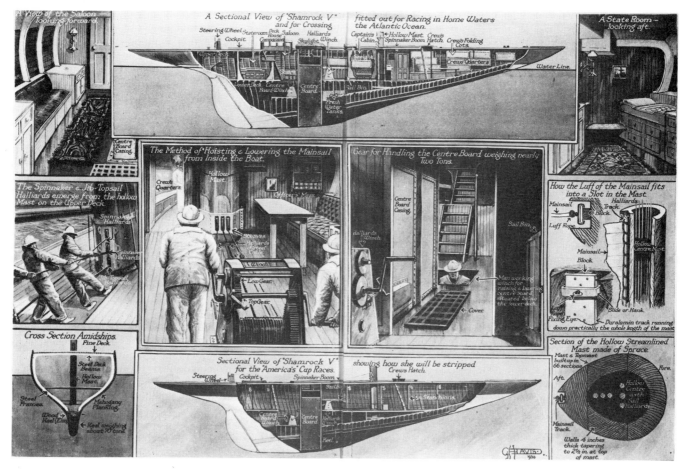

Labels within the illustration:

A View of the Saloon looking forward

A Sectional View of 'Shamrock V' and for Crossing the Atlantic Ocean — fitted out for Racing in Home Waters

Steering Wheel · Stateroom · Deck House · Saloon · Halliards · Captain's Cabin · Hollow Mast · Crew's Spinnaker Boom · Hatch · Crew's Folding Cots

Cockpit · Companion · Skylight · Winch

Upper Deck · Lower Deck · Centre Board Winch · Centre Board · Sail Bin · Water Tanks · Crew's Quarters · Water Line

A State Room — looking aft

The Method of Hoisting & Lowering the Mainsail from Inside the Boat

Gear for Handling the Centre Board weighing nearly Two Tons

How the Luff of the Mainsail fits into a Slot in the Mast

Crew's Quarters · Hollow Mast · Officer's Mess · Sheaves · Halliards · Winch · Low Gear · Top Gear

Centre Board Casing · Halliards Winch · Sail Bin · Man working winch for raising & lowering centre board situated below the lower deck · Cover

Mainsail Track · Halliards Block · Luff Rope · Mainsail Block · Hollow Centre Mast · Slide or Hank · Fixing Eye · Duralumin track running down practically the whole length of the mast

The Spinnaker & Jib-Topsail Halliards emerge from the hollow Mast on the Upper Deck

Spinnaker Halliards

Cross Section Amidships. Pine Deck · Steel Deck Beams · Hollow Mast · Mahogany Planking · Steel Frames · Wood Keel (Elm) · Keel weighing about 70 tons

Sectional View of 'Shamrock V' for the America's Cup Races showing how she will be stripped

Steering Wheel · Cockpit · Spinnaker Boom · Crew's Hatch · Sail Bin · St. Stanchions · Centre Board Winch · Centre Board · Keel

Section of the Hollow Streamlined Mast made of Spruce. Mast & Topmast built up in 66 sections · Fore · Aft · Hollow Centre with Sail Halliards · Mainsail Track · Walls 4 inches thick tapering to 2½ in. at top of mast

G. H. DAVIS. 1930

Above: Shamrock V shown in section by an Illustrated London News artist for racing in home waters, for crossing the Atlantic, and for racing for the America's Cup. She lost four races in a row./Illustrated London News

Right: Enterprise, with her light-weather genoa./Beken

design was influenced by his experience in building to the International Rule – Shamrock's more rounded sections both forward and aft appeared more typical of an International Rule boat than one built to the Universal Rule – and it was acknowledged that there was probably little difference in hull speed between the two. The rigging and gear, however, was another matter. As a writer in the American magazine Yachting commented they 'fell far short of the perfection attained in Enterprise.' He then went on to list some of the imperfections, and rather startling they seem.

'The challenger was lacking in variety and number of light sails, and she had but few winches for setting a trimming sail, or for adjusting the tension on the headstays or shrouds. Even the main sheet was trimmed by hand, and it took nearly the whole crew to get it in when she was on the wind.* There was no tack on the gooseneck, or tackle to tack the mainsail down as the sail and halliard stretched.' Even the purchase on her backstays was rope, not wire. As Nicholson himself stated, 'the tendency of the rules in Britain has been to discourage experiment and originality along these lines,

*In fact, the main sheets of all the Big Class were trimmed by hand.

and unfortunately Shamrock V paid the penalty.' He did not make the same mistake twice.

But rig and gear apart it was really a matter of the better man winning. Building to the J-Class rating had brought in a new era of yacht design, and Vanderbilt complemented this breakthrough by bringing in a new era of management and sailing skill. But the skipper and crew of the British yacht were professionals, paid by the yacht's owner to race as best they could. Crew members who raced in her during the 1930 series say she was not a particularly happy ship during the races and that the afterguard were amateurs in the worst sense of the word. They did not know what they were doing and disregarded the advice of the professionals. As none of the afterguard is alive today, there cannot be a reply to these charges. But it was a long time ago now and whatever the truth of the allegations the fact is that Enterprise was a superior boat in every way. Vanderbilt, who should have known, simply said that the reasons he beat the British challenger were that 'the luff of Enterprise's headsails, owing to shorter headstays and greater tension thereon, sagged off to leeward much less than Shamrock V's and that Enterprise's lighter mast – 4,000 pounds against the 6,350 pounds of Shamrock's – and Park Avenue boom proved superior to Shamrock's spars.' He also said

that when sailing free, *Enterprise* used better sail combinations and had a greater variety to draw on, and that her afterguard 'had a greater appreciation of the value of tacking to leeward.'

The challenge over, one of the many British yachting correspondents who bewailed yet another failure put the blame fairly and squarely on the attitude with which the challenge had been organised. 'The latest attempt to win back the America's Cup has resulted in a dismal failure, and now yachtsmen are trying to explain this failure away by talking a great deal about the power of the 'almighty dollar', just as if they had only now realised that such a power existed! All this talk is rather nonsense, for anyone who has given a thought to the American sportsman's viewpoint must know perfectly well that your American never does anything half-heartedly. He is never lukewarm. Mr Bobby Jones takes his golf very seriously, Mrs Helen Wills-Moody has made lawn tennis her life's study, and Mr Harold Vanderbilt does not exactly go boat-sailing because summer is the closed season for fox-hunting.'

The writer then went on to challenge the accepted British attitude towards the amateur helmsman. 'Mr Andreae and Sir Philip Hunloke are the only two men in the whole country to whom we can turn for examples of the amateur's skill in first-class racing yachts . . . Is it reasonable to believe that (they) are unique? I think not. The other amateurs should be given an opportunity – they should have been given that opportunity long ago. In America they would have had their chance, but in this country we cannot depart from the old regime which is painfully senile, we cannot say, as they do in America: "We believe blank is the right man for the job; let us give him a try" . . . In this country Jones once luffed Robinson, and thus for evermore they are estranged . . . Again, in this country we've always heaved and hauled on our sheets ten men at a time. Winches, we say, are unseamanlike. "New fangled gadgets," we bluster. "Dammit, sir, they destroy the old traditions of the sea. Man power is the right power." Blowing out our chests we bawl, "one, two, three – pull!" and haul our sheets in far too flat, while the Americans, Norwegians and Swedes, trim their sheets on nice little winches and sail away.

'No. Our failures in the America's Cup and British-American Cup races cannot be attributed solely to the "Almighty Dollar", for if we had but looked astern we would have discovered that we were towing a host of foolish conventions, traditions and personal differences far heavier than any bucket ever made.'

Whether the British yachting fraternity took due note of this broadside or whether the writer had simply felt the 'wind of change' on his cheek it is impossible to say, but 1930 proved to be a watershed for British yachting. In America the new decade welcomed a new breed of yacht; in Britain it acknowledged as well a new breed of yachtsman.

But 1930 was also the year for *Lulworth* – one of the old timers – with a professional skipper, Archie Hogarth, at her helm. *Shamrock V* might have been the yacht to win the most races before she departed for the 'other side' but in the close circle of the professional racing hand it was *Lulworth*'s year. It was a windy summer which must have favoured the larger, heavier yachts and *Lulworth* beat *Shamrock V* no less than four times before the challenger had to withdraw from the racing circuit to prepare for her Atlantic crossing. *Lulworth* started forty-six times that year – only *Cambria* had more with forty-nine. Of those *Lulworth* won eleven, came second in six and third in four.

Although *Lulworth* was never converted for the J-Class, 'Skipper' Albert Stroud's vivid picture of life aboard* that summer conveys well what it must have been like to live and race in one of the Big Class. Many of the men who sailed in her subsequently crewed on the Js.

'It was early breakfast on racing mornings, and you had no more meals until racing was over and the decks and varnish work all cleaned, the latter with fresh water and chamois leathers to remove any trace of salt. You rose at 5 am when racing, scrubbed down and "chamoised up", cleaned the brasswork, and then breakfast. After breakfast it was the caterer's job to go ashore, shop, get the mail, and get the "baby" filled (the four gallon stone jar for the crew's beer). Licensing hours were waived for this as it was a recognized thing all round the coast, and he had to be back on board by nine o'clock to have the dinghy stowed on deck and be ready for a ten o'clock start. For the rest of the crew it was clear the fo'c'sle and get all the sails for'rard from the sail lockers aft, then they were stowed in their respective places in the fo'c'sle ready for changing when necessary, for in those days there were three jib topsails to change at various points in the racing. The "baby" for going to windward in a stiff breeze, or the "medium" if the wind eased at all, and when rounding the mark to go on a reach, it was the "long rope" that was set. In addition there was, for light winds the "yankee" jib topsail, or the bowsprit spinnaker, and the spinnaker itself

*from an unpublished manuscript.

which was boomed out for running before the wind.

'All these sails were in place down in the fo'c'sle, the spinnaker having its sheet already fastened to a deck stanchion for security, for when it was set up straight from below, and if the sheet wasn't fast, it *could* take charge in a breeze. As soon as sails were changed they went straight below where they were "made up" ready to set again on the next round. To make them up they were stretched through from the fo'c'sle, through the saloon and to the after cabin, being stopped up with rotten cotton for after being set again in "stops" they were easy to break out when the sheets were hauled on. When running before the wind, it was possible to have a quick sandwich and a glass of beer, the sandwiches being of cheese and about an inch thick and this would be your lot until the racing finished.'

'Everybody aboard had their racing positions, and these they kept throughout the season. There was the first and second mastheadsman, and the bowsprit-end man. The mate was always for'rard when racing, watching the trim of the sails, the second mate was aft by the skipper, the bo'sun on the mainsheet, the two stewards on the preventer backstays. Myself, I was on the port runner, my opposite number being on the starboard runner, then there were the port and starboard staysail-sheet men, and the port and starboard jib-sheet men. To each of these it was the job to belay the sheets or tackles round the cleats. In this way, there was no confusion when the vessel tacked. It was the same when setting sail, certain crew members had special jobs. It was my

job to belay the peak halyards, and also the jib topsail halyards, to insert the spinnaker boom in the socket on the mast, and to belay the spinnaker outhaul when the spinnaker was set, and then across to the mainboom guy and take the guy tackle right for'rard in light weather to keep the mainsail right out to the rigging when running, and if the bowsprit spinnaker was set, to sit on the lee rail and watch that sail all the time, passing signals by hand to the crew on the winch whether to haul in or slack off, according to how the light airs came.

'The helmsman – if he's keen and knows his job – can tell whether a boat is doing its best, and here are some instances from my days in *Lulworth*. As runner man, when you got your runner tackles down to what was thought a good pitch, the Skipper would tell you to put a mark on the tackle where it came through the sheave, and on occasion he would say, while we were sailing in a breeze "ease that tackle just an inch", a tricky job with the mast depending on it, it meant just taking the hitch off the cleat, and easing each turn on the cleat by just that fraction with your hand without taking any turns off. Or to the mate he might say "take half a turn off the lee rigging screws, Mr Mate", and when you tacked, he would take half a turn out of the other side. Now to the ordinary man he wouldn't think that one inch on a runner tackle, or half a turn on a rigging screw would make any difference, but to a man who had got the "feel" of the vessel via the steering knows whether a vessel is being "pinned" too much. It's the same with using shifting ballast, you can tell whether or not a vessel is "dragging" along or whether she is

Above: One of the great racing skippers, Archie Hogarth, aboard *Cambria*, 1928. His mate, George Francis, is at the wheel. Later, Hogarth became skipper of *Lulworth./Stroud*

easy or hard on the helm. Such are some of the attributes of a good skipper, especially in racing.'

Racing was a tough occupation – the men's fingers were often split by the Italian hemp ropes which were used, and they would bind them up with tarred twine, tar being a very effective antiseptic . . . From the time the season started either at Harwich or on the Clyde (later, the season always started at Harwich) at the beginning of June to when the season closed in September at Dartmouth there were well over forty races to compete in, each one being about forty miles in length. In addition the crews covered up to about 1,500 miles in passage sailing from one regatta to another. The pay was meagre though it was boosted by prize money if the yacht gained a flag – £1 for a win, 15s for second place, 10s for a third, plus 5s starting money and 2s 6d grub money. The basic pay was around £3* a week, and out of that a crew member had to pay for his food which cost about 8s 6d. The caterer was appointed by the men, and much depended on him being good at his job. A bad caterer meant less money in the crews' pockets or poor food – and sometimes both. Sometimes, an owner would help out as Skipper Stroud recalls: 'Lulworth's owner was a Mr Paton, who was a big food-importer, and I, being the caterer for the crew, was called into the saloon one day. He asked me the type of bacon I bought and in what quantities. I replied that I generally bought it in rashers as it was more economical to buy rashers already sliced, than buy it in the piece and leave the cook to slice it, for he would not be able to slice like a

*They were paid only during the summer months, though during the winter they were sometimes paid a retainer.

Above: Westward and *Britannia* passing the guardship, HMS *Warspite*, during Cowes Week, 1930. *Britannia* won this race, bringing her total of victories to 200. It was the last year that she raced with her gaff rig. / *The Field*

Left: One of the rare fatal accidents: *Lulworth* (on right of picture) sinking the 12-metre *Lucilla* during Cowes Week, 1930. Immediately ahead of her is *Cambria*. One of the crew of *Lucilla* was drowned./*Beken*

Above: The J-class weren't the only ones to lose their masts. This stump is all that was left of *Lulworth*'s when she was dismasted in 1928./*Lay*

Right: Candida, in the Solent. /*Beken*

machine. I also told him that we bought fore-hocks for boiling joints when passage making. The outcome of this conversation was a note from Southampton station to collect a full side of bacon . . .'

The crew for *Lulworth* and for the other Big Boats came mostly from the East coast fishing villages of Tollesbury, West Mersea and Brightlingsea but there were others who came from the Itchen area, Chichester harbour, and the West Country. The Stroud family came from the Kent fishing town of Whitstable and as many as six brothers sailed on the Big Boats at one time or another. One season three of them were in *Britannia*, and later three of them sailed in *Shamrock V* to America for the America's Cup races. The Diapers were another prolific and well known professional sailing family, 'Dutch' Diaper, the skipper of *Shamrock V* when Richard Fairey owned her, being probably the best known. Albert Turner, Ted Heard, Captain Williams of Sopwith's two *Endeavour*'s, Fred Mountifield of *White Heather* and then *Velsheda* – he was known as grizzly bear because he was so gruff – Bill Randall, Archie Hogarth – 'he never looked behind him when racing' – were all experienced skippers who were widely known and respected, and who

mostly chose their crew from their home towns or by word of mouth. They might not have had quite the same charisma as the earlier generation of professionals like Sycamore and Charlie Barr but they were tough and competent seamen nonetheless.

But though 1930 was *Lulworth*'s year, it was also her unluckiest. During a West Country regatta she lost a man overboard and was forced to retire. Luckily, the man was a strong swimmer and he managed to grasp a judiciously thrown lifebelt. *Lulworth*'s dinghy, launched in the miraculous time of sixteen seconds, soon had him on board again. Then, later in the season at Cowes, she ran down and sank the 12-Metre *Lucilla*. She was running free at the time and going like a train, a full point by the lee, when *Lucilla* tacked across her bows. *Lulworth*'s iron martingale went through her starboard bow and she sank immediately with the loss of one hand. After this tragedy the racing rules were altered but it is an indication to the modern reader of the power and speed and size of the Big Boats of the 1930s.

The wind was strong throughout Cowes Week that year – it was what was known as 'Britannia weather' for the Royal Yacht needed a real blow to get her going – and it was during the Week that *Britannia* won her 200th race, a remarkable achievement which was cheered loudly by the crowds watching from the shore. She might not have been winning as many races as she had done in the past but to the spectators *Britannia* still ruled the waves. The win was also extremely popular because the King, having recovered from his extended illness, was on board again. Even Queen Mary went for a sail that year, something she never normally did, for she hated the sea and was invariably seasick.

So strong was the wind that the first day's races had to be cancelled and on another only *Westward* – 'wild as a hare under a whole mainsail' – and *Candida* started, and only *Candida* finished, thus enabling yachting writers again to lament the passing of the old racing yachts with their sturdy rigging who could race in a summer gale without fear that the whole lot would fall down on top of them.

This criticism was somewhat unfair as the Big Class had always been prone to losing spars – *Britannia*, in the year she came out, got through no fewer than three lower masts, one topmast, two bowsprits and a gaff – but no doubt the increasing expense of repairs was as much a contributing factor to the owners' caution as the lightness and complexity of their boats' rigging and spars. The full force of the Depression had not yet struck. But the signs of it were there for all to see like thunder clouds on the horizon.

The Mechanical Ship

Enterprise *had been accused of being a mechanical ship . . . As for winches, after looking over our '57 and one varieties' (actually I think we had twenty-three) and comparing his (Nicholson's) meagre few, we both agreed that if we had too many, he had far too few.*
Sherman Hoyt's Memoirs

The era of the J-Class in the United States began on 20 May 1929 in the Broad Street Club in New York when members of the America's Cup committee of the New York Yacht Club met to discuss yet another challenge from Sir Thomas Lipton.

Lipton's last challenge, held over because of the outbreak of war in 1914, had been in 1920. Now, nine years later, yachting in Britain had just begun to rid itself of the effects of patronage and inherited wealth that had lingered on after the end of the War. In America the tradition had always been more democratic, less bound by convention and class distinction. By 1929 it was common for amateur owners to steer their own yachts.

Yacht design, too, had advanced dramatically with the introduction of the marconi rig and its accompanying jib-headed sail plan. We call it bermudan rig and think nothing more of it, but it must be remembered that in those days the abandonment of the gaff rig must have been as revolutionary in the yachting world as the supplanting of the square rig by the fore-and-aft had been. It certainly caused almost the same quantum leap in efficiency when sailing close to the wind.

The trend on both sides of the Atlantic after the War was away from the vast yacht with its enormous complement of paid hands. Sailing gradually became more of a popular pastime, not just the exclusive sport of the very rich. The new type of owner was a man who knew the sport through sailing a smaller class boat and just because he was wealthy enough to buy a larger vessel that didn't mean he intended giving up the fun of steering it himself. Inevitably, this trend meant that more yachts were built but that they were built smaller. On the American side, the huge schooners began to fade from the racing

scene so that by the end of the decade, on Western Long Island Sound for example, only *Resolute* and *Vanitie* of the Big Boats remained, though the M-Class (up to 54 feet on the waterline) and the 12-Metres still flourished, along with the smaller classes like the forties, tens, and Larchmont 'O's.

These factors must have been in the minds of the committee that hot spring day when, after agreeing to the conditions of the match, it voted to accept the challenge with both boats being built to rate as J-Class under the Universal rule. It was also agreed that both challenger and defender must be built to Lloyd's A1 scantling rules, thus ensuring that the challenger was strong enough to cross the Atlantic on her own bottom and that the defender did not have any unfair advantage in weight.

It was then decided that two syndicates should be formed to build prospective defenders. Winthrop Aldrich agreed to head one and Junius Morgan took on the leadership of the other. All thought it essential that there should be at least two boats from which to choose the defender and both *Vanitie* and *Resolute*, although now rigged to rate with the J-Class, were banned from competing because of their light construction.

Though not eligible to enter the official trials, both *Vanitie* and *Resolute* proved useful trial horses for the newly built Js. Both had long and distinguished racing records and they must certainly have helped to carry on the tradition of Big Boat racing in American waters through the 1920s, giving crews, skippers, and owners the experience of handling outsize yachts, and presumably also keeping alive public interest in this size of boat. They therefore have a part to play in the story of the Js.

Resolute, the successful 1920 Cup defender, was handled in her early racing days by Charles Francis Adams but was subsequently sailed by a later owner E. Walter Clarke of Philadelphia who raced her when she was schooner rigged and when she had been converted to a J. His son Sidney took over for her last two seasons. *Vanitie*, built in 1914 to defend the Cup, was bought by Gerard Lambert in 1928. Lambert – it was he who

Left: Whirlwind's double-headed rig proved a failure, so she reverted to the conventional triple-headed rig. It did not improve her performance. Note the canoe stern./*Rosenfeld*

45

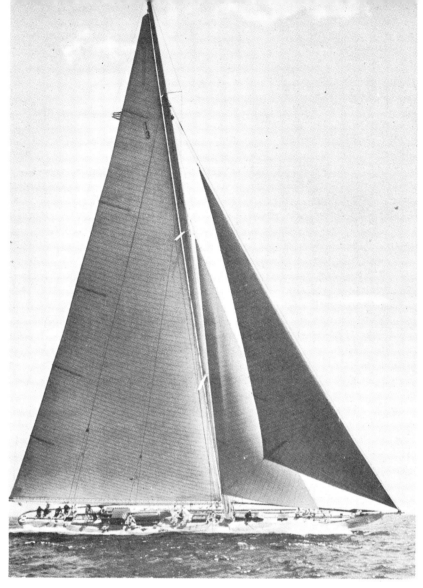

coined the phrase 'great racing contraptions' – was a newcomer to the sport, but he learnt quickly and later bought an unsuccessful 1930 Cup defender *Yankee* and took her to England in 1935.

Both *Vanitie* and *Resolute* were outstanding yachts and were keen rivals over a very long period of time. Between 1914 and 1933, for example, they raced for nine seasons in 143 races. As gaff rigged sloops, *Resolute* raced in forty-six races and *Vanitie* in forty-eight. They were then rigged as staysail schooners and sailed in fifty and forty-six races respectively. While gaff rigged, *Resolute* won thirty-four of her races to *Vanitie*'s thirteen, but when their rig was changed *Vanitie* won twenty-six races to *Resolute*'s thirteen. Finally, they were rerigged as cutters, but again *Vanitie* proved superior winning thirty-three races to *Resolute*'s six.

Resolute faded from the racing records very early on in the 1930s and though *Vanitie* kept racing much longer (and occasionally, very occasionally, beating *Weetamoe* who was her only rival between the challenges of 1930 and 1934) neither yacht was a match for the new Js. On her first trial race *Enterprise* beat the identically rated *Resolute* by over four minutes, and two days later, when she met her again in a strong breeze, she beat her by just under ten minutes. And when *Enterprise* raced against *Vanitie* she beat her in light winds by $2\frac{1}{2}$ minutes even though *Vanitie* was a bigger boat and carried 500 sq ft more sail.

Far left top: *Vanitie* with
Gerard Lambert at the wheel.
Designed by Gardner she was
generally regarded as one of the
most beautiful yachts ever
built./*from* All out of Step *by
Gerard Lambert*

Far left bottom: First race for
the 1930 Cup candidates off
Glen Cove. From left to right:
*Enterprise, Vanitie, Whirlwind,
Resolute* (with the race
committee tug to windward
of her), and *Weetamoe./The Field*

Left: Starling Burgess (left)
with Harold S. Vanderbilt.
Burgess designed or co-
designed three Js: *Enterprise,
Rainbow* and *Ranger./Rosenfeld*

Below: Harold S. Vanderbilt at
the wheel of the defender./*The
Field*

The results surprised some of the old salts who had been predicting the previous winter that both *Vanitie* and *Resolute* would thrash the new Js. The new boats would be too heavy, they said, and they would lack stability. They did not have sufficient sail area to drive their heavier and larger hulls in the light breezes that blew during the summer months. Again, it was a case of the experts underrating the power of the new high aspect ratio sail plan.

The designer of *Enterprise*, Starling Burgess, had no such doubts however. At the beginning of the season he handed to the yacht's helmsman Harold – 'Mike' to his friends – Vanderbilt an envelope marked 'not to be opened until after the finish of the first race with *Resolute*'. As *Enterprise* crossed the line after the first trial, Vanderbilt slit open the envelope and read under the heading 'Light to moderate breezes. *Enterprise* wins by upwards of three minutes on a 20-mile course'. In fact, *Enterprise* won by 4 minutes 8 seconds over a 25.8 mile course.

It was the Aldrich syndicate which built the successful defender, and a powerful and immensely rich group of men they were: Harold Vanderbilt, Vincent Astor, George F. Baker, George Whitney, Floyd L. Carlisle, and E. Walter Clarke. The Morgan syndicate, which built *Weetamoe*, consisted of equally important people: George Nichols, J. P. Morgan, Cornelious Vanderbilt, Arthur Curtiss James, George T. Bowdoin, Henry Walters and Gerard Lambert. Between them, the two syndicates must have owned quite a slice of the wealth of the country. They were then joined by two more syndicates. One, led by Landon K. Thorne, and supported by Alfred Loomis and Paul Hammond, built *Whirlwind*, designed by Francis L. Herreshoff, Nat's son. The other was a Boston syndicate organised by John Lawrence, with fellow Bostonians Charles Francis Adams, Chandler Hovey, and the designer Frank Paine. They built *Yankee*, the only American J the British ever saw in their waters.

The syndicates were formed and boats built before the effects of the great Wall Street crash began to be felt. There was a lot of money about and people were prepared to spend it. Enormous sums were laid out by all four syndicates, though more was spent on *Enterprise* than on the others. It was estimated that well over three million dollars was expended on the four Js! A vast sum for those days. Such extravagance was never seen again.

Vanderbilt both managed and skippered *Enterprise* and had a Scotsman, George Monsell, as his sailing master. His afterguard, as he called his team of consultants, consisted of Aldrich, Sherman Hoyt, C. 'Bubbles' Havemeyer, and the yacht's designer, Starling

Burgess. *Weetamoe*'s skipper was George Nichols who had J. Christiansen as his sailing master. With him as afterguard were John Parkinson, A.H. Eustis, Robert N. Bavier, and *Weetamoe*'s designer, Clinton Crane. *Whirlwind* was skippered by Paul Hammond with John Muir as his sailing master. Landon K. Thorne managed the boat, and with them was W. Chamberlain. Finally, *Yankee* was managed by John Lawrence but skippered by either Charles Francis Adams or C. Raymond Hunt, with Olsen as their sailing master. The afterguard consisted of Lawrence, Frank Paine, and Chandler Hovey. All four yachts were manned by professional crews of Scandinavian origin, though a few members came from fishing communities on Deer Island off the New England coast.

Both *Weetamoe* and *Enterprise* were built at the famous Herreshoff yard, and *Yankee* and *Whirlwind* at Lawley's of Boston. *Enterprise* was first into the water, on 14 April 1930, and this may well have been a factor in her becoming the successful boat to defend the Cup for she was certainly tuned

Left: Weetamoe under full sail. /*The Field*

Below: Enterprise on a reach. This shows well how the curve in the mainsail is maintained by the Park Avenue boom./*The Field*

up and racing much earlier than her rivals. *Whirlwind* was next in the water, on 7 May, despite being badly delayed by the Lloyd's inspectors who insisted she should have an entirely new set of lower scantlings which had to be rushed through and fitted. This in turn delayed the launching of *Yankee* because *Whirlwind* blocked her way in the building shed, but she eventually entered the water on 10 May, the same day as *Weetamoe*, whose launching had also been delayed when she got stuck on the ways.

Once commissioned, the yachts were put through a rigorous tuning up programme before beginning the series of informal trial races which were only a prelude to the official observation races from which the defender was to be chosen. These early races showed that *Weetamoe* was the light weather boat, that *Enterprise* was very fast to windward in moderate airs, *Yankee* was the best all round boat, and *Whirlwind* was a flier with started sheets. But *Weetamoe* slacked up when the wind was over ten knots, *Enterprise* could not reach or run quite as well as the others, while *Whirlwind* was easily beaten by the others when close-hauled whatever the strength of the wind. The American yachting magazine, *Rudder*, commenting on these early races, stated: 'unless *Shamrock V* can climb

to windward in a moderate to fresh breeze at something better than eight knots, run down the wind under spinnaker at an eleven knot gait, and reach with ballooners at a speed of thirteen knots, she might as well stay on the other side.' *Shamrock V* couldn't.

Interest in the four boats was intense in American yachting circles. Nothing quite like it had been seen since the great building spree for the last Dunraven challenge in the previous century. And this interest was stimulated by the sensible attitude of the syndicates. The secrecy normally associated with the building of Cup defenders was abandoned. When the models of all four yachts were put on display in the New York Yacht club *Rudder* pointed out that this was 'practically unheard of in the history of this big race, and it certainly seems to indicate an improvement in sportsmanship.'

John Lawrence, *Yankee*'s syndicate leader, even went so far as to make a statement giving full details of the syndicate's plans. 'Our design has been laid down at the George Lawley and Sons yard at Neponset. The bulb angle frames are being bent and the bronze plating moulded into shape. The lead keel has not been laid because it will be moulded into the bottom of the frames and plating during construction – a very old method, but

Top right: Whirlwind, just after her launching. She was a total failure./*Boston Globe*

Bottom right: Yankee, 1930, making good time. /*Paul Hammond*

Below: Weetamoe in a stiff breeze./*Rosenfeld*

one not usually employed in boats of this character. Our boat will be 125 ft overall, 84 ft on the waterline, 22 ft 4 ins in beam, and a 15 ft draft. Our lines are rather full and fair. Designer Paine has drafted a very simple, well balanced boat with a lot of power and of a very strong construction. We hope to carry 7,500 sq ft of sail. The design for the 165 ft mast is at Lawley's, the wood and glue selected and work will begin on this big stick this week, while the needed sails to start the season have been ordered from Ratsey and Lapthorn of City Island.'

Lawrence didn't mention that *Yankee* would also have two masts as the Cup committee had decreed that no boat would be considered as a candidate for the observation races unless she had a replacement mast. This, as *Rudder* pointed out, was a sensible provision when it was remembered that no less than five of the previous eleven yachts that had been built for the America's Cup had lost their sticks during their trials: *Columbia* in 1899, *Shamrock II* and *Constitution* in 1901, *Shamrock III* in 1903, and *Resolute* in 1920.*

There was something of a scramble for men and materials, both of which were limited, and Vanderbilt records that much of his canvas – four mainsails, one staysail, one

*They were not to be the last either, for both *Ranger* and *Endeavour II* were dismasted before they raced for the Cup in 1937.

jib, three jib topsails, two spinnakers, two ballooners, one genoa jib, one storm trysail and a small or passage staysail – was ordered from Ratsey and Lapthorn a good two months before the yacht's keel was laid, thereby anticipating the rush of orders from the other three syndicates. Planning like this was the mark of Vanderbilt, the outstanding organiser and three-times successful defender of the America's Cup.

Whirlwind was of composite construction, but the other three were built of Tobin bronze, a traditional American method of constructing Cup defenders. It gave a bottom of glassy smoothness, and was both light and strong. Some said the only reason *Whirlwind* was not built of it too was the shortage of expert craftsmen and lack of bronze (*Yankee*'s plating alone used 55,000lbs). *The Boston Globe* went so far as to print an article asserting – perhaps half-jokingly – that the Vanderbilt syndicate had deliberately bought up all the bronze plate in order to force Francis Herreshoff into building his boat in other, and inferior, material. But Paul Hammond denied that the *Whirlwind* syndicate were short-changed and said that Herreshoff preferred working on a wooden boat and deliberately chose composite construction.

Ratsey's made the canvas for all four contenders; Merriman Bros. supplied all the blocks and turnbuckles, and many of the winches; and the Plymouth Cordage Com-

Top right: Weetamoe's sail plan. /*Crane*

Bottom right: Weetamoe's lines. She was *Enterprise*'s closest rival to defend the America's cup in 1930./*Crane*

Below: Enterprise's mainsail spread out in the Ratsey and Lapthorn loft. More than a mile of Egyptian cotton went into the sail which weighed about a ton and measured about 5,000 sq.ft./*Geoff Hammond*

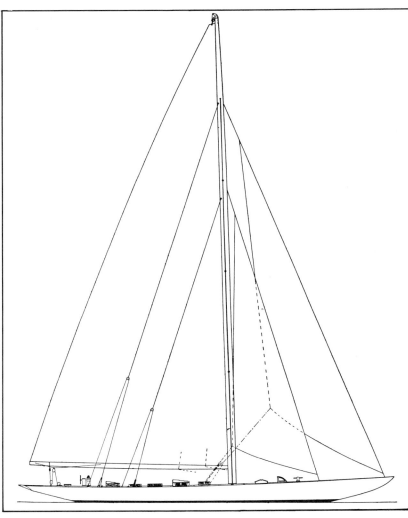

pany twisted most of the running rigging, including the mainsheets, 90 fathoms in length.

An interesting comparison between the four boats was made by the naval architect, Charles Nedwick, and the author is indebted to him for the following description:

'*Weetamoe* is the narrowest, *Yankee* the broadest, *Whirlwind* the longest, *Enterprise* the shortest. On *Whirlwind* the bottom of the keel runs practically parallel to the load waterline from the heel of the sternpost to the middle of her length. Rounding up from that point, it runs in almost a straight line to the forward end of the water line. A large area of lateral plane is secured by a profile of this type. Nevertheless it has, to my mind at least, several disadvantages. First, with the large lateral plane comes an increase in wetted surface and, consequently, great frictional resistance; second, the greater area tends to make the yacht slow in stays and also hard to balance. Due to the large area of lateral plane, the designer has omitted a centreboard.

'At the other extreme in the matter of profiles is *Weetamoe*. Disregarding the rudder, she has a profile that is practically a triangle, with a straight line from the after end of the waterline to the bottom of the keel and thence a line which is slightly convex, and then slightly concave to the forward end of the waterline. A lateral plane of this type has

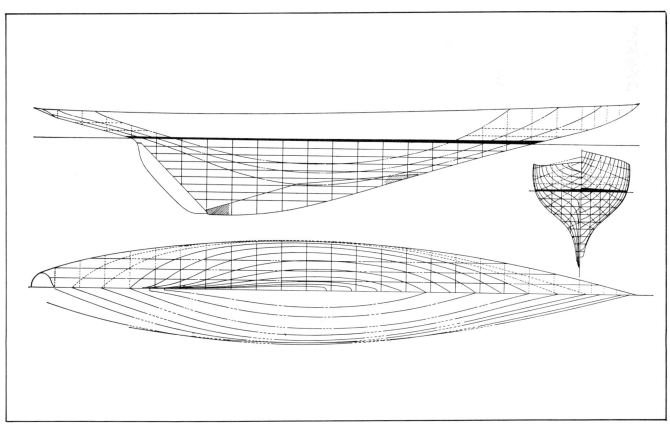

Right: Like the other four Js, *Enterprise* was being continually altered and adjusted to improve her performance. This shows the changes made to her rigging during the season./*from* Enterprise *by Harold Vanderbilt*

minimum wetted surface and consequently lessened skin friction. The tendency is for such a boat be quick on her helm. To ensure enough lateral resistance for windward work, a centreboard, working through the lead keel, is fitted.

'*Yankee*'s profile is essentially of the same type as that of *Weetamoe*, except that her keel line runs straight and with a slight drag for about twelve feet from the heel of the rudder post. It then sweeps up to the waterline in a graceful curve, first convex, then concave. *Yankee* has a small centreboard fitted just forward of her rudder post.

'*Enterprise*'s underwater profile resembles that of *Whirlwind*, but with her forefoot cut away to a greater extent. This should make her quicker in stays and easier to handle than *Whirlwind*. One advantage of this type of profile over that of *Weetamoe* and *Yankee* is that the centre of gravity of the lead ballast is low, making for a stiff boat. *Enterprise*, like *Weetamoe*, has a centerboard working through her lead keel.*

'Above water, the outlines of the boats are much alike. The total length of the overhangs is about 43ft, half forward and half aft. *Weetamoe*, *Yankee* and *Enterprise* have the usual type of transom stern while *Whirlwind* has a canoe stern, as have several other yachts from the board of her designer. On *Yankee*, *Enterprise* and *Whirlwind* the sheer line is almost straight, while *Weetamoe* has decidedly more sheer than is usual in yachts of her type. It may be said here that sheer does not make a boat either fast or slow but has much to do, if properly designed, with making a good looking boat.

'The transverse sections, drawn from a study of the models, show *Enterprise* as being the most normal in respect and by "normal" I mean that her sections are more like that of the previous Cup yachts (such as *Vanitie* or *Resolute*) than those of the three others. With her light displacement, large sail area and general hull form, *Enterprise* should be at her best in from light to moderate weather, and a very good "drifter".

'*Whirlwind*'s underbody gives the impression of power. The bulk of her displacement is high, which means hardbilges. It must be remembered that she has the largest displacement of the quartet, having almost thirty long tons more than *Enterprise*, the smallest boat. Her wetted surface must be considerably more than that of the others. Taking all of these things into consideration, and remembering that her sail area is practically no greater than that of the others, it

may be said that she would be put to it to defeat any of them except in extremely heavy weather.

'*Yankee* and *Weetamoe* show a decided similarity in the type of their transverse sections. Both have the bulk of their displacement lower than the other two. As closely as can be judged from the models, their sections approach the type of the smaller racing classes – slack bilges amidships, with full sections at the ends. This generally produces a "softer" boat, but one that has nice lines when heeled and that is apt to behave well in a seaway. Both of these yachts, judging from their longitudinal profiles, must have the centre of gravity of the outside lead higher than do *Whirlwind* or *Enterprise*. This has its effect on their stability.

'In comparing *Yankee* and *Weetamoe*, it is odd that the widest and the narrowest boats of the four should show the general similarities that they do. Due to her wide beam, *Yankee* is probably the most powerful of the lot, next to *Whirlwind*. Her easy lines should make her a better all round boat than the latter, at her best in moderate to heavy going and yet a boat to watch in light weather. *Weetamoe*, the narrowest of the quartet, should have the least stability. Nevertheless, with her greater length and larger displacement, she might be just as powerful as *Enterprise*. Like that yacht, she should be at her best in light to moderate weather.

'All four yachts have the so-called Marconi mainsails and all except *Whirlwind* have double-headed rigs.* Hollow booms and masts, built up of clear western spruce on fir, are used. *Enterprise* and *Whirlwind* each has, in addition to the wooden stick, a hollow mast built of duralumin, which combines great strength with lightness.'

It is interesting that of the four designers only Francis Herreshoff experimented by building to the limit of the rules, 87ft on the waterline. Clinton Crane, *Weetamoe*'s designer, thought the other designers were influenced by the fact that the only boats afloat that resembled the new Js, *Resolute* and *Vanitie*, were only 76 feet long, and that building to the limit of the class might mean that the boats would be undercanvassed. Crane comments that he wasn't entirely persuaded by this argument and, in fact built *Weetamoe* rather larger than the members of the syndicate really desired. When Charles Nicholson, the British designer of *Shamrock V*, went and looked at *Weetamoe*

---

*In fact she had two centreboards as a small one was placed aft, mainly to help stability when running.

*Nedwick is wrong about the rigging of the Js, or maybe it was a printer's error. All the Js, except *Whirlwind*, had the conventional triple-headed rig. *Whirlwind* started off with a double-headed rig but abandoned it.

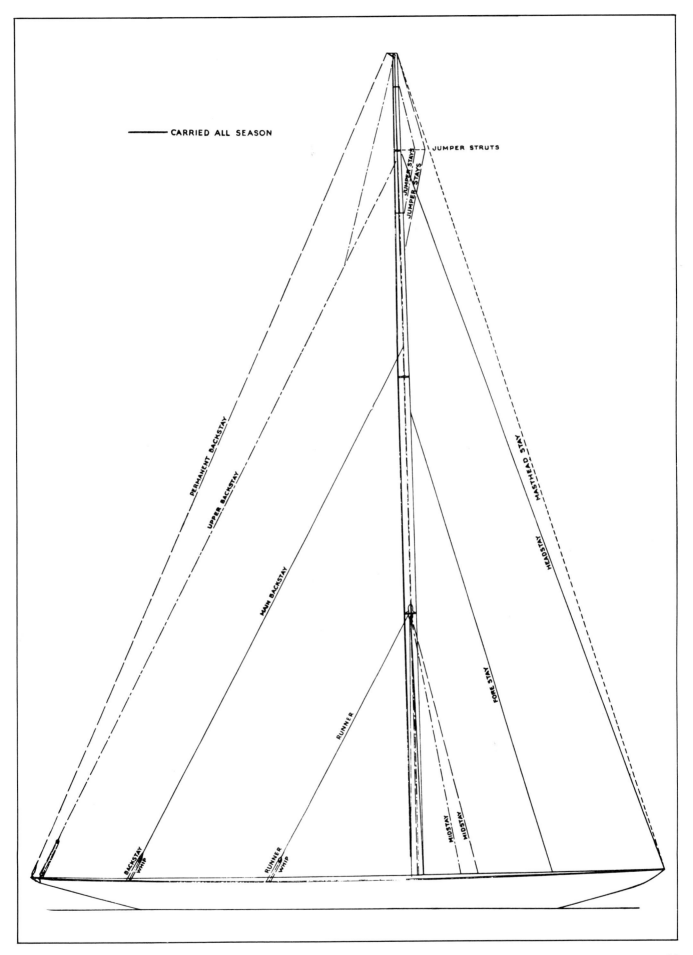

CARRIED ALL SEASON

JUMPER STRUTS

JUMPER STAYS
JUMPER STAYS

PERMANENT BACKSTAY

UPPER BACKSTAY

MAIN BACKSTAY

MASTHEAD STAY

HEADSTAY

RUNNER

FORE STAY

MIDSTAY
MIDSTAY

BACKSTAY
WHIP

RUNNER
WHIP

after *Enterprise* had been chosen to defend the Cup he declared her to have the best hull of all the American Js.

Whirlwind was a double-ender because Herreshoff wanted to follow the lines of *Istalena*, the successful M-Class yacht he had designed. In fact, *Whirlwind* was announced to be an enlarged version of *Istalena*, and was built almost entirely of American materials. Her steel framing came from Pennsylvania, her mahogany from South America, the pine in the deck and spruce in the mast and spars from the State of Washington, and the black walnut in the rail and deck trimmings from Indiana. All the metal fittings, including the steering gear, were specially designed and, as the designer pointed out, in many cases quite different from those used on any previous yacht.

Without a doubt *Whirlwind*, quite apart from her canoe stern, was the most radical of the Js, and forty-five years later Olin Stephens declared her the most interesting of the quartet. In designing her Francis Herreshoff followed the time-honoured system of his father by making more than 250 blueprints for the builders to follow. But though he followed his father's system in building, in actual design the younger Herreshoff moved right away from the elder Herreshoff's conservatism in design. All kinds of new gadgets went on board while the other three Cup boats used tested designs and proven methods.

One innovation, however, the steering gear, was probably the main reason *Whirlwind* was out of the running so early in the season. It made her a fearsome creature to keep on course in anything of a wind and once it threw a helmsman clear over the wheel! Paul Hammond, who must have helmed her more than anyone, said the steering worried him all summer and that at first the syndicate had thought the boat unbalanced. 'We changed the position of the mast six times and that was time lost when we should have been racing,' he said. 'She was a bitch to steer. I used to start her and then Landon Thorne would take over and within half an hour he was worn out. Herreshoff made the fanciest gear you ever saw, it looked like a mass of gold all that wonderful brass gearing'.

'Even though her chances are slim,' *Rudder* commented, '*Whirlwind* must be regarded as the outstanding yacht of the season in expressing originality, ingenuity and skill in design and construction. No Cup yacht or any other racing craft ever carried quite so many new fangled ideas as L. Francis Herreshoff has installed on the Thorne-Hammond yacht, and anyone who has the opportunity should certainly examine carefully this marvellous creation. The wizard of Bristol has been "outwizarded" by his own son, and he admits it. Only a few can be noted. The shroud plates on the mast have their screws clutching the wood in different directions, so the pull is distributed. Not only

Top right: Whirlwind as she started the 1930 season, with a double-headed rig./*The Field*

Bottom right: The tangs on *Whirlwind*'s mast which helped to spread the load. They were one of the many innovations introduced by L. Francis Herreshoff who designed her. /*Paul Hammond*

Below: Whirlwind: another view of her double-headed rig. /*Yachting*

has the yacht a permanent backstay, made possible by her long canoe stern, but her single runners which lead far aft can be thrown off easily by the man at the wheel, by a very clever tripping arrangement from the cockpit, an invention which designer Paine immediately adopted for the *Yankee*. In her early races the *Whirlwind* carried only a staysail and single jib, but this rig can be discarded for the conventional three sail head gear without a change in the headstays. It is not surprising therefore that the younger Herreshoff should be the receiver of many flattering notices, and that the owners of the *Whirlwind* should have received a relatively high bid for their yacht for the season of 1931.'

About *Whirlwind*, Herreshoff himself commented: 'although there is very little variation possible in the complete and complicated rule under which these boats are built, I believe that *Whirlwind* embodies more of the recent developments in small boats, such as those in the R and Q Classes, than the other three boats in the class. I have therefore tried to make *Whirlwind* appear longer, lower and racier than the type of boat normally expected under the Universal Rule, with its present requirements of freeboard.'

Certainly her lines attracted Uffa Fox who wrote: 'the profile is very pleasing to the eye, the stem sweeping down to the keel in a very sweet line, and to a man who, like myself, believes that a pointed stern is a logical ending

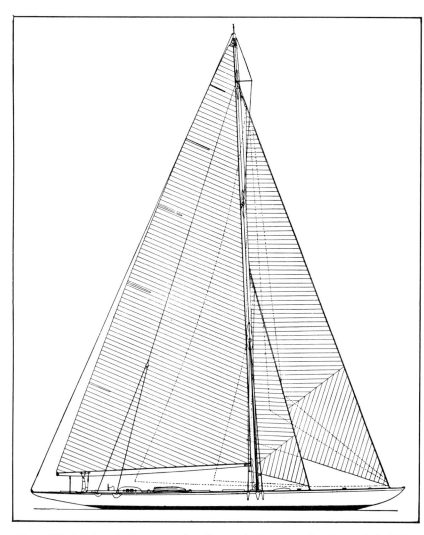

*Above: Whirlwind's sail plan.
| Herreshoff*

gear needed altering. He could have been right but unfortunately no one tried to put matters right, not even her new owner Mr Pynchon, the owner of *Istalena*.

Apart from her hull design, *Whirlwind* was ahead of her time with her double-headed rigging, and this again was a natural development from *Istalena*. But Uffa Fox thought that Herreshoff was really groping for the single-headed J of the future. Writing in 1935 he said: 'In spite of being designed six years ago, *Whirlwind*'s sail plan is the most advanced, her mast and its rigging is most instructive and interesting . . . there is no stay aft from the forestay, this proving that *Whirlwind*'s rig was designed as a single headsail rig, the rig that in years to come will be adopted by all the J-Class racers, in spite of the enormous strain it will put upon their masts, and the difficulty the crews will have in handling and sheeting such a sail.'

Whirlwind's afterguard, however, did not appreciate the advanced thinking of her rigging and reverted to the triple-headed rig in an attempt to get her properly balanced. Sadly, Uffa Fox's prediction that, since she was built as stoutly as *Britannia* she would last as long as the royal yacht had did not come true, for she was broken up in the very year he published his predictions about her.

Enterprise, the yacht chosen to defend the Cup, was at the opposite end of the design scale to *Whirlwind*. She was the shortest where *Whirlwind* was the longest, and she was utterly conventional. Even so Burgess had quite a few problems to overcome and like all the other designers he was breaking new ground. For it must be remembered that no class boat the size of the Js had ever been built before. The M-Class was the nearest, but the M-Class were only 50 to 54 ft on the waterline, a lot smaller than the 75 to 87 ft of the J-Class, and though similar hull lines could be considered it was not just a matter of 'scaling up' an M-Class design. The matter is a complicated one but, to refer to the problem of the rigging only, Clinton Crane expresses clearly the task a designer faced when building on such a large scale: 'Weights of similar structures, of the same material, vary as the cube of the dimensions; but a bridge, or a spar, or a beam, will only carry a weight which varies as the square of the dimensions. For instance, a bridge 100 ft long will weigh 1,000 times as much as a bridge 10 ft long if every member has been increased in the same ratio; that is, the length, width and thickness of every member of the larger structure must be ten times that of the smaller one. But this 100ft bridge, which weighs 1,000 times the 10ft bridge, will only carry 100 times what the smaller one will carry, and that must include the weight of the bridge itself. This

for all vessels, her stern is a joy to behold.'

Unlike the other designers, Francis Herreshoff raced only once with his creation. Perhaps he knew from the start that she was a failure, and, after the fame and success of his father he must have been bitterly disappointed with her performance. The boat was entirely his own design despite a *New York Times'* report early in 1930 which stated: 'once more Nat Herreshoff has played a hand in the defense of the America's Cup . . . After the younger Herreshoff, who as a draughtsman went to work in Boston independently of his father had drawn the preliminary plans for *Whirlwind*, one of the defense boats, he took them to his father who went over them. At the family home in Bristol, R.I., father and son held a long consultation.'

In fact, according to Paul Hammond, the younger Herreshoff never asked his father's advice at all, one reason being that they didn't get on all that well. There were indications, however, that old Nat knew what was wrong with *Whirlwind* but said nothing about it until after she had been eliminated from the trials. Then he wrote to Hammond advising him not to have her 'cut up', asserting that she was the right length and only her steering square-cube relationship places a definite limiting size on every kind of structure. There is therefore a definite limit of size beyond which no bridge can be built.

'In the case of yacht spars and rigging, the main loading is caused by the sails and varies as the square of the dimensions, but there is still a large load due to the weight of the masts and rigging themselves. In a 6-Metre the sail loading at 30 degrees of heel is roughly $5\frac{1}{2}$ times that due to the weight of the mast and rigging; in a 12-Metre $3\frac{1}{4}$ times, and in a J $2\frac{1}{4}$ times. The total load on the mast of a twelve at 30 degrees angle of heel is five times as great as on a six, not four times as it would be if the load varied as the square of the size, as a twelve is about twice the size of a six. The load on the mast of a J-boat is $5\frac{1}{2}$ times the load on a twelve metre's mast, though here again the load should be four times if it varied as the square of the size. These figures make it obvious that as boats get larger the masts and rigging, to be of equivalent strength, should increase faster than the cube of the dimensions. However, in the formula which was adopted in 1930 for the classes J, K, and L, the different weights are still based on the cube of the size and the formula then adopted produces a much lighter mast than is allowed in the International Rule. In fact if you apply this formula to a 12-Metre, the mast would weigh less than 700 pounds although the International Rule requires a mast to weigh 1,000 pounds.'

It was, therefore, not just a matter of scaling up. In considering what size they were to build their yacht, the Aldrich syndicate had to decide whether to follow the normal pattern of building to the maximum waterline length of the class, or whether the sheer size of a J introduced other factors which overruled that criterion.

In deciding the length of *Enterprise* Burgess first obtained as much information as he could about the strength of winds to be expected off the racing area – and the reports went back over twenty years of racing. From what was known as the relation between wind velocities and the speeds of *Resolute* and *Vanitie* with their J-Class rigging, it was estimated that *Enterprise* should be designed for maximum performance at about 10.75 knots, as the winds during the period when the Cup was to be raced rarely exceeded 12 knots and *Enterprise* therefore could rarely be expected to sail at her maximum speed. Burgess, by means of tank tests, then calculated that for this speed the waterline length of 80 ft was the most efficient. This meant the rule allowed a displacement of 128 tons and 7,583 sq ft measurement for the sail area.

Above: The wooden mast and spreaders with which *Enterprise* started the 1930 season./*from* Enterprise *by Harold Vanderbilt*

Vanderbilt agreed with these calculations and was against building to the limit of the rules. 'I favoured this short waterline boat because I could not see how a boat 87 ft on the waterline or only 3.1 per cent shorter than *Reliance*, which defended the Cup in 1903, could be adequately canvassed in light breezes with 55 per cent less sail.'

He proved to be right though for the wrong reasons. *Enterprise* almost certainly won the right to defend the Cup not because of her length but because of her duralumin mast and the superior organisation of afterguard and crew, and because the longer boats, *Yankee* and *Whirlwind* were not properly tuned. The 1934 trials produced very different results, with *Yankee* very nearly earning the right to defend.

Enterprise went through all her preliminary trials with a wooden mast. Then, six weeks after her launching, Vanderbilt stepped the new duralumin mast designed by Burgess's brother, Charles Paine Burgess. It was 162 ft in length and weighed a mere 4,000 pounds, very much lighter than any wooden mast built. Because of the limitations in width and thickness of duralumin plates available at that time the mast was constructed with a double skin. It was twelve-sided and riveted together with between 80,000 and 100,000 rivets. To give the mast sufficient play it was stepped in a watertight steel tube filled with a liquid resembling quicksilver.

In torsion and transverse strength the mast was satisfactory; but it was much too flexible fore and aft, and the designer found that the headstays and backstays had to be adjusted with every alteration of wind direction, or change of sail. 'We have learned,' Burgess commented, 'that it is just as important to trim the stays as it is to trim the sheets themselves.'

The delicate task of keeping the mast in the boat created a new job on *Enterprise*, that of 'mast nurse'. Burgess took on this job, handing over to Aldrich his original assignment of navigator. To help him with his task he had an instrument called a shunt dynamometer which had been developed and used by engineers for bridge construction. This measured accurately the strain on the headstays and backstays and they could therefore be set up with great precision. This was done below decks with the aid of eight winches, and it took the crew many weeks of hard training to perform their tasks efficiently.

The duralumin mast made a marked improvement to the yacht's stability. Vanderbilt also noticed that *Enterprise* seemed much

easier in a seaway with the lighter mast, and that her improved stability reduced pounding. 'She felt like a different boat,' he wrote, and certainly her performance against her chief rival, *Weetamoe*, improved from then on. Crane, *Weetamoe*'s designer, commented that 'the mast is a miracle, and it is a miracle that you can keep it in the boat!' In light airs the lower spreaders could be folded – 'cock-billed' – to stop any interference with the setting of the genoa.

If the manufacture and stepping of *Enterprise*'s new mast had its problems, the building of the ordinary wooden masts for the other Js was not a simple matter, if only because of their excessive length and the speed with which they had to be built. Bror Tamm, who was in charge of the spar shop at Lawley's where *Whirlwind* and *Yankee* were built, ran into plenty of headaches when he was asked to build both the primary and spare mast for *Yankee* as well as the primary mast for *Whirlwind*. 'It was a heck of a job to get the wood,' he is quoted as saying in an interview with Charles Mason (*Sail* magazine 1974). 'It was all spruce and the best 40ft sections had all been shipped to Japan. It was almost impossible to find anything much over 30ft and I wouldn't take stock with less than 12 annular rings per inch. If it had any more,* the tree had grown too fast and might be weak.'

Scarfing the wood together to get the 170ft lengths was the next step. Scarfs were made carefully to be twenty times the thickness of the wood. It took a dozen men two months to glue all the sections together into full-length pieces $2\frac{1}{4}$ inches thick. Each piece weighed between 500 and 800lbs, took twenty men to lift, and bent like a piece of spaghetti. After the pieces had been glued, the 170ft lengths were carried by hand to the mill to be cut and planed by machine.

But well before the wood went through the power moulder, Tamm was confronted with the problem of the design for the masts: '*Yankee*'s mast consisted of eight pieces, four corner pieces and four stave or side pieces that were the sides of the mast. Francis Herreshoff had actually advised against using this system, saying that it would be too weak. Still, that is the way the mast had been designed, though no one was quite sure how to build it. Francis Herreshoff had designed an even more complicated section for *Whirlwind* with an internal track running down the aft side. It was a darn good idea but difficult to do.'

Putting the pieces through the moulder created a problem as the mill was nowhere

Below: The wonder mast that probably won *Enterprise* the right to defend the America's Cup. It was made of duralumin. /*from* Enterprise *by Harold Vanderbilt*

*he must have meant less.

near long enough. Doors were opened, gaps aligned, and eventually the 170ft lengths were fed through the moulder via an alleyway, the entire length of another building, and then up over another building 25ft high and 50ft wide! Yankee's mast was glued on one side of the shed and Whirlwind's on the other. Forty-five horses were set up in a row on each side and aligned exactly so that the first stave piece could be tacked down on them. All the pieces were then glued to that piece, first the two corners, then the side pieces, then the top corners and finally the fourth side.

'Yankee,' Bramm explained, 'had an exposed track and we could build her with the back of the mast flat on the horses. But Whirlwind, with her internal track, had to be built upside down with the forward, or tapered side, facing down. This meant all the horses had to be shimmed up exactly to get the proper taper. It had to be precise to $\frac{1}{64}$ of an inch or better. We practised putting the pieces together and I checked everything from every angle a hundred times to make sure the joints were perfectly matched. For once you had started the glue, there was no turning back and if something went wrong, the whole thing would be ruined and it would have to be thrown away.'

To make certain the pieces were exact, a boy with a torch was sent up the inside of the mast with a roller skate strapped to his back! It was a lengthy and costly business. A wooden mast cost $15,000. On the other hand, Enterprise's duralumin mast was estimated to have cost between $25,000 and $30,000! The difference in cost between Enterprise and the British challenger was remarkable. According to Yachting World the hull of Shamrock V cost £18,000, and all her sails, gear and spars another £10,000 or so. The bronze and steel hull of Enterprise cost £50,000. Add to this the cost of her eight mainsails at £24,000, her thirty others sails at £25,000, her mast costing £8,000, her crosstrees £2,000, two extra masts £6,000, her Park Avenue boom £2,500, extra rigging £5,000, and ·it will be seen that Enterprise's cost was at least £100,000.

Under the rules for the 1930 challenge it was agreed that the crew for each yacht was limited to 31, including the afterguard which usually numbered five. Most of the crews were taken from the yachts belonging to members of the various syndicates. Monsell chose the majority of his from Vanderbilt's two yachts, Vagrant and Prestige, and some came from Valiant, which belonged to Winthrop Aldrich.

Another of the rules allowed the contestants to have their winches – and the men working them – below deck, and in fact all

Below: Looking forward on the starboard side of *Enterprise.* The centreboard winch – painted white – is on the left and on the extreme right is the main sheet spool. Note the slatted floor to save weight. / *The Field*

1930

five yachts involved in the 1930 series were complete shells with no accommodation of any kind. *Enterprise* split her twenty-six man crew – 'the black gang' they were called – nine below deck and 17 above. On deck the sailing master was in charge of the main sheet, the backstays and runner while, the first mate was responsible for the trimming of the head-sheets and sail changing, and the second mate passed any order below to the third mate who was in charge of the crew below decks. Naturally, all four acted on orders from the afterguard.

In *Enterprise* each crew member had a number assigned to him and was given a jersey with that number on it which corresponded with the number of his station. If a change was subsequently made in station the man need only change his sweater, allowing the number of the station to stay constant. Each man had a specific task alloted to him. Numbers one and two were on the jib winches, and three and four on the staysail winches. Five and six were on the main sheet drum, and seven and eight on the starboard and port backstay winch respectively. After a tack, it was the job of numbers one and two to set up the lee jib winch, numbers three and four set up the lee staysail winch before number one slacked off the weather jib winch and three slacked off the weather staysail winch. When the jib was lowered one and two would go on deck, and when the staysail was lowered three and four would go on deck. They would then stay there until ordered either to hoist the sails again or to make them up. All work was done in complete silence, and when not working the crew on deck would lie on the weather side when close-hauled or wherever was best to trim the boat.

The pay for the crews was generous by the standards of the day. The log of the *Weetamoe* syndicate records that they paid their sailing master $6,000 on a year's contract, payable $500 monthly. In addition there was a $1,000 bonus for him if *Weetamoe* was selected to defend the Cup plus a further $1,500 if the Cup was successfully defended. The first mate received $3,500, and racing money, the second mate $2,800 and racing money, and the three quartermasters $120 monthly and racing money. The ordinary seamen received $110 monthly plus racing money. Each man got $5 for a start, $10 for a win, and there was to be a bonus of $150 if *Weetamoe* was chosen to defend the Cup and $250 if she raced and won.

The afterguards of the four Js usually consisted of the skipper/helmsman, the navigator, relief helmsman, and two specialists for the rigging and setting of the sails. In *Enterprise* Vanderbilt was the skipper, with

'Bubbles' Havemeyer as his assistant helmsman. Winthrop Aldridge, as recorded, was the navigator and Sherman Hoyt and Starling Burgess the sail and rigging experts respectively.

It was Vanderbilt who really coined the word afterguard, and who ran his boat by committee. This was quickly adapted by the other Js to a greater or lesser extent but unfortunately for the British it was something they could never manage to accept.

Before the start of a race Vanderbilt would be at the helm and he, Sherman Hoyt and Havemeyer would decide what light sails to set. Aldrich, meanwhile, would be noting courses to steer and these were checked by Havemeyer who would then put them on the steering stand. Aldrich was also responsible for the starting watch, and he and Havemeyer would come up with the starting formula. Then Vanderbilt, advised by Hoyt and Havemeyer, would decide on his starting tactics. Finally, Vanderbilt, or Hoyt advised by Vanderbilt, would decide when to break out the light sails.

Once they had started Vanderbilt would remain at the helm if the first leg was on the wind, but would relinquish the wheel to Havemeyer if they were running free. Either way Hoyt advised, though obviously Vanderbilt had a say if Havemeyer was steering. The trim of the main sheets was supervised by Sherman Hoyt who also watched the trim of the head sails. Vanderbilt advised about the main sheet when Hoyt was steering and also when Havemeyer was at the helm. On the wind, it was Havemeyer's job to watch the course and sail changes of the other yachts, and to tell Vanderbilt if they tacked, while Hoyt was in charge of supervising the changing of the head sails, though this was always done with Vanderbilt's approval. There was also a committee on tactics which consisted of Havemeyer, Aldrich and Hoyt. When Vanderbilt was at the helm going to windward he invariably followed the committee's suggestions so that he could concentrate fully on steering. The committee, presumably not to distract him, always met out of his hearing!

Sailing free had more or less the same organisation except that Aldrich took Havemeyer's job of watching the other yachts and the committee of tactics consisted only of Vanderbilt and Hoyt. While rounding a mark Vanderbilt took the helm and trimmed the main sheet, and Havemeyer saw to it that the backstay and runner men were at their posts and that the main sheet was eased correctly when necessary. Hoyt was in charge of the headsails and it was Aldrich's job to time all the other yachts rounding the mark. Burgess was also given the permanent assignment of watching and advising on the mast, stays and rigging; Aldrich navigated and kept the log book; and Havemeyer kept the sail book. There wasn't much time for anyone to enjoy the view.

Enterprise was truly a team boat and was meticulously run, and it is perhaps worth noting at this point what Clinton Crane had to say about the running of *Weetamoe*, *Enterprise*'s main rival. George Nichols, the skipper of *Weetamoe*, knew, he said, the racing game from A to Z. 'He knew not only how to sail a boat but when to tack and when not to tack, what the best position was, and how to get the most out of a boat. The one weakness that George had was that he did not find it easy to rely on his afterguard. I think he took more out of himself on *Weetamoe* that summer than any other skipper, and largely because he did not make use of those of us who were with him and could have taken some of the load off his shoulders.'

Crane also made some interesting and valid points about the function of the afterguard. After remarking that a really good navigator may make all the difference between winning and losing, he goes on: 'The skipper must further be assisted by someone who is competent to adjust the staying of the mast to see that it is properly standing at all times. This is a matter of constant supervision and cannot be assumed to be set right once and for all, particularly in boats like the Js which were so lightly rigged in proportion to their size as to be much more delicate than most smaller racing boats.

'Although sail trimming is primarily under the direction of the skipper on the wind, he must be helped by some competent member of the afterguard who can be in more places on the deck, and observe sails from more different angles, than is possible for the man at the wheel. Off the wind, where sail trimming is of great importance and the sheets must be constantly trimmed and eased for the best results, many good skippers turn over the wheel to a relief helmsman and themselves personally supervise the trim of the sails. There must always be on board a relief helmsman competent to take over and relieve the skipper, although some skippers – and Charles Francis Adams is one of them – hold the wheel all through the race.'

But to race a J was only part of the task. To administer the whole operation of keeping her running and sailing was much more complicated. The yacht and her crew had to be constantly supplied with every need – Vanderbilt had no less than seven mainsails that season – and every eventuality had to be anticipated and catered for. Both crew and yachts had to be kept in first class trim. To see that this was done all four Js

Above: A fine line-up of all the American Js during the 1930 season./*Yachting*

had accompanying vessels which housed the owners or the crews, and carried spare sails and additional equipment. The *Weetamoe* had a steamer called the *Emblane* in attendance along with two power boats, *Magistrate* and *Momo*. *Yankee* had what was called a navy barge named *Dandie*, and also two power boats, *Doodle* and *Gypsy*. *Whirlwind* had as her tender a schooner called *Minas Princess* and a power boat called *Twister*. Vanderbilt's own diesel yacht, *Vara*, was the headquarters for the afterguard of *Enterprise* and in addition she had no less than three other craft to look after her and her crew: *Corona*, which housed the crew and was a useful stationary sail locker; *Mut*, for ferrying the crew, and for victualling; and *Bystander* which towed *Enterprise* to the starting line and stood by in case she was needed. Each syndicate probably had upwards of a hundred men working to keep each J sailing as fast and as efficiently as possible.

As the summer progressed the odds lengthened against both *Whirlwind* and *Yankee*, and the choice for the defender of the Cup lay between *Enterprise* and *Weetamoe*. During July there were ten official observation races, at the end of which *Weetamoe* came out on top by only one point. Things looked bleak for Vanderbilt and he knew that unless he could beat his rival consistently during the New York Yacht Club cruise races which followed the observation races *Enterprise* stood no chance of being chosen. He reckoned he had to improve *Enterprise*'s performance by up to two minutes over a thirty mile course, and he set out to do just this. The following week *Enterprise* was taken back to Bristol where some alterations were made to her rigging.

New winches, including additional main backstay ones, were also fitted. The shunt dynamometers, which Vanderbilt had ordered, arrived and as previously mentioned these proved of great benefit to Burgess and the afterguard who no longer had to guess how much strain could be put on the rigging. The instrument was simple, but effective and accurate, and consisted of two hooks on adjustable arms one at each end of the instrument which were attached to one side of the stay or sheet. A deflecting lever at the centre held the device in place and when pressure was applied to it it deflected the stay or sheet sufficiently for the angle of deflection to be measured against the amount of force needed to cause the deflection. Tables computing the amounts of strain did the rest. Vanderbilt records that eventually the backstays were able to carry as much as 15,000 pounds load when racing.

The New York Yacht Club cruise and the Eastern Yacht Club cruise are still today two of the most important dates for American yachtsmen. They are very different from the Englishman's concept of a regatta – they aren't run with the public in mind at all but solely for the enjoyment of the competitors and any shipborn spectators who care to follow them. The races are organised so that the yachts race from one yachting centre to another, well away from the shore.

Even so, the social pleasures were the same, and everyone was out for enjoyment. 'Sociability and yachting are synonymous,' one contemporary yachting article said. 'Picture a fleet rendezvous at Marblehead, Newport, Larchmont or at some other famed yachting center. The commodore in his high-powered tender is making the rounds, welcoming newcomers and extending the courtesies of the port to yachtsmen from near and far. Glistening paint, shining brass, immaculate white flannels and the gay sports attire of smartly clad women vie with the beautiful club house surroundings for a place in the sun. Everyone seems to know everyone else. Friendly hails come across the sheltered inlet as the day is closing.

'The boom of the sunset gun is a signal for the lowering of the flags. Down comes the ensign and burgee on the yacht club pole, and all over the harbor other flags disappear, to be followed immediately by the glimmering of dozens of masthead lights. Lights gleam too from port lights and flicker softly from plate glass cabin windows. Soon everything will be ablaze with the witchery of lights. Already tenders are making for the club's landing. The ladies are going ashore for dinner. A lone yacht is tooting her horn for the patient club launch. The captain evidently is disinclined to lower his own dinghy . . .

'On the club verandahs shore folks are mingling with yacht people. Some wear the usual light, summery things, while those who have just come in from the race boats are clothed in almost anything. Over there is a girl in pink overalls with a sailor's jacket under them. The older woman she has engaged in conversation has apparently been sailing too for her white dress clearly shows that it is wet through and through.

'A girl comes across the verandah dragging a duffle bag. She affects an ultra short skirt, woollen socks, sneakers and a rough blue sweater. Her hair is drawn back from her face by means of a multi-coloured scarf. She too is wet, and as she walks along each shoe emits a distinct squelsh, leaving tiny pools of moisture in her wake. She stops to chat with a group of fashionably dressed women who have just come in from contract bridge on one of the larger yachts. All know each other and light laughter greets the sallies between the sailor lass and the bridge players.

'Upstairs the men are gathering about, discussing the day's racing. One can hear the clink of ice in glasses. They are going over the protests of the regatta . . . like the women the men range from spotless white flannels down through dungarees and old bathing jerseys. The man in the corner boasting a three-day growth of beard balancing the cocktail shaker is an absurd picture. Bare-footed, his disreputable pants and stained sweat shirt make him look for all the world like a beachcomber, but he is the center of interest. He owns the finest sailboat in the club and the largest power yacht which is used solely as a tender to the former. He himself may look nondescript but his crew and his boats are flawless.

'One of the most delightful experiences is dining aboard . . . it would be a shame if an ugly coast guard cutter came along and caused us to heave overboard the liqueurs we thought had passed out of existence in 1918 . . . When night comes we sit down to cards. We bid outrageously. The captain turns on the radio and we dance.

'An almost countless number of sail and power boats followed the cruise in its entirety and many of them had distinguished guests

Below: This table is from *Weetamoe*'s log and shows how meticulously each sail was tried out and its performance noted. */NYYC*

List of Sails tried out on 24 July				
Sail	*Marking*	*Wind and Force*	*Hours Used to Date*	*Remarks*
Mainsails	No. 2 Sudan	10—S.W.	37	Our best sail, fine up to 15 mph.
	No. 1 Sudan	15—S.W.	63	Our poorest sail, rather full
Jibs	D, high clew	10—S.W.	New	Looks well—results doubtful
	E, low clew	12—S.W.	New	Looks well—results doubtful
	B, high clew	15—S.W.	43	Getting old—used up
	F, small, high clew	16—S.W.	New	Too little change in size to be of any value
Jib Topsails	No. 2 Long, A	10—S.W.	6	Too full and light on foot. Returned to City Island for recut
	No. 2 Long, B	14—S.W.	New	Too full and light on foot. Returned to City Island for recut
	No. 2 Very long, A	14—S.W.	New	May flatten out with use, now too full
	No. 3 Long, A	15—S.W.	6	Very good sail
	No. 4	16—S.W.	4	Very good sail
	No. 1 B	15—S.W.	New	Very good sail
	Large Balloon, B	10—S.W.	New	Very good sail
Staysails	C	10—S.W.	New	Very good sail
	B	14—S.W.	28¼	Getting old and blown out
Jib Topsail	Small Balloon, B	14—S.W.	New	Very good sail
Spinnaker	Large, B	14—S.W.	New	Very good sail

Above: Enterprise's Park Avenue boom. A steel jackstay secures the mainsail to the slides. As the sail is carried over when tacking the slides travel along the transverse runners. Holes in these runners allow pegs to be inserted to control the distance the slides will travel which in turn controls the curve of the mainsail.
/Rosenfeld

aboard. A great many of the windjammers were attended by power tenders on which the crews lazily waited the finish of each day's racing before being called into service. In some of the races the crews and skippers were rigged out to represent pirates, young ladies or what-have-you, much to the amusement of the other crews. Sherman Hoyt in one of the races was dressed in bright red trousers with beret to match and at his side was slung a knife that might easily have graced the form of Captain Kidd.'

Life was obviously fun and casual, except when you were asked to dinner – then you wore proper clothes and remembered your table manners. The days of obligatory white flannels and yachting cap were over, for the sailors, at least. 'At most of the larger regattas on the East Coast this year the only fully clothed people on board the boats were the members of the professional crew,' *Rudder* commented in its September 1930 edition. 'The owner and his guests were almost universally clad in either just old, dirty canvas trousers (usually shorts) or simply the lower half of a very much abbreviated bathing suit. Evidently the "sun-bathing" rage has hit our sailormen with a vengeance. On the other hand the motor boat contingent are more formal. White ducks, white flannels, natty blue yachting coats and, of course, the ever present yachting cap are much in evidence even at outboard regattas on inland lakes. There's one bone we have to pick with these men. It is the spreading use of a yachting cap at the upper end and "plus fours" at the lower end of a yachting costume. A most ludicrous combination.'

After finishing behind *Weetamoe* on the race between New London and Newport on

2nd August 1930, *Enterprise* did surprisingly well on the 4th when the Js raced from Newport to Mattapoisett. The wind was blowing at 25 knots from the south-west and Vanderbilt expected to be last as it was thought that both *Yankee* and *Whirlwind* were the fast boats in strong winds. But *Weetamoe* lost a man overboard and, although he was recovered, she was soon out of the running, and *Enterprise* beat *Whirlwind* by twelve seconds coming in twenty seconds behind *Yankee*. Vanderbilt put down this improvement in running and reaching in a strong breeze to a change in the trim of his yacht. The use of his genoa jib also helped. It was during this race that the Cup boats sailed the fastest leg of any race: 16.25 miles in one hour, 18 minutes at 12.46 knots. *Enterprise* then went on to win the next four races, yielding only the final one to *Weetamoe*. This was an impressive showing, and was certainly enough to erase the edge that *Weetamoe* had gained during the observation races. They could be said to have entered the official trial races on even terms.

After the New York Yacht Club cruise, *Enterprise* was again taken back to Bristol. Her rigging and sails and trim had by now been perfected but Vanderbilt wanted to test a number of new gadgets before the official trials began on August 20th. In particular he wanted to test the Park Avenue boom.

This extraordinary device had been designed by Starling Burgess and his brother Charles after Vanderbilt had discussed its possibilities the previous winter. Its object was to give the bottom few feet of the mainsail its natural curve and therefore make it aerodynamically perfect. Triangular in shape, it was four feet at its widest point which was approximately a third of its length from the mast. Flush with the top of the boom were transverse metal tracks about a foot and a half apart to hold the foot of the sail to the curve required. The curve was changed to suit the strength of wind, the change being effected by taking out the stop pins near the end of each track and replacing them in holes that allowed the track to move into the required position. On *Enterprise* there were three series of these holes as well as the centre hole. Each line of holes was painted a different colour for easy identification and came to be called after the similarly coloured lines on the map of New York subway system: Seventh Avenue, Times Square shuttle, and Lexington Avenue. In addition to its aerodynamic advantages the width of the boom to windward of the sail stopped the down draft of wind – or end spill as it is called.

Fully rigged the Park Avenue boom weighed 2,330 pounds, several hundred more than the conventional boom *Enterprise* had previously been carrying, but this additional weight was more than compensated by the boom's efficiency in making the mainsail a near-perfect aerofoil. Two men could easily walk abreast down its whole length, hence its name! Bill Stephenson, the son of *Velsheda*'s owner, recalls that the whole Stephenson family, plus friends, had lunch atop their boom while racing at Le Havre in 1935!*

The new boom proved to be a success and Vanderbilt went on to experiment with a smaller rudder. This, too, was successful once he'd got used to the different way *Enterprise* handled, and it saved as much as one per cent of wetted surface.

The trial races were brief. Only three of them were held. The yachts again raced in pairs and for the first two races *Enterprise* raced against *Weetamoe*, and *Yankee* took on *Whirlwind*. *Enterprise* won both her races against *Weetamoe* as *Yankee* did against *Whirlwind*. In the third trial *Enterprise* raced against *Yankee* and though the race was abandoned through lack of wind it was not called off before *Enterprise* had proved her superiority in light weather by being a mile ahead of her opponent when the time limit expired. It was at any rate a good enough performance to satisfy the selectors: *Enterprise* was subsequently chosen to defend the Cup.

There was a lot of comment amongst the yachting fraternity at the swiftness with which *Enterprise* had been chosen, and the old rivalry between Boston and New York came briefly to the fore again. This is well caught in an anonymous letter in the October issue of *Rudder*: 'In view of the fact that *Yankee* is definitely not a "drifting machine", I am not at all surprised that the committee entrusted with the job of picking the America's Cup defender should have made its choice of *Enterprise* after running off a few thoroughly unsatisfactory matches in light airs. Anything to make a Boston entry appear at great disadvantage when it comes to the America's Cup contest. Signed: Bostonian.'

In retrospect, however, it was not *Yankee* which was *Enterprise*'s closest rival but *Weetamoe*, and the comment of the grand old man of American yachting, Nat Herreshoff, perhaps sums up best the general feeling about the two competing Js. 'They're about as different as two boats could be, but there doesn't seem to be much difference in their speed, so I guess they're both wrong.'

*The Park Avenue boom was not a brand new invention as many people thought – Dr Manfred Curry had written articles about its use in small boats – but it was the first time that such a boom had been built and used in a large yacht.

The Flying Millionaires

There were those who scoffed at the new-fangled ideas of these 'flying millionaires', saying that Fairey and Sopwith between them were making the sport too expensive. That was nonsense, for as Dick once said to me: 'If a fellow starts asking how much it costs to go yachting, the answer is that he can't afford it!'

Anthony Heckstall-Smith

The 1930 season in Britain had seen no less than eight Big Boats racing together, the largest number ever seen – a magnificent sight but it also caused the rule makers a good deal of concern. For those eight yachts were the products of no less than three separate classes. *Britannia, Lulworth, Westward* and *White Heather II* were handicap yachts; *Astra, Cambria* and *Candida* were racers built to the International Rule of 1928; and *Shamrock V* was built to the American Universal Rule. At the beginning of the season the first four had been alloted time allowances which meant they raced level amongst themselves and gave seven seconds per mile to *Candida* which sailed to her rating (24 metres) as did *Cambria* (23.7 metres) and *Astra* (23.8 metres) who received 1½ seconds and one second respectively from *Candida*. Finally, *Shamrock V*, as we have seen, began by receiving five seconds per mile but ended up giving time.

None of this proved very satisfactory. The first group had to be handicapped on merit, while the second group were rated according to their rule. But if the first group had been handicapped on the basis of any rule it is doubtful whether they would have won a race, and certainly their commercial value as racers would have been practically nil. But as long as handicapping by merit continued there seemed no good reason why anyone should spend money on a new yacht. Those who might have been tempted to build to the International Rule to challenge the members of the second group were discouraged from doing so because they knew they would never be able to challenge for the America's Cup which was now controlled by the American Universal Rule.

Something had to be done and the Yacht Racing Association took the following steps before the 1931 season began: they abolished handicapping by merit; they agreed with the Americans to adopt the Universal Rule for all yachts over 14½ metres and to use the International Rule for everything under; and they framed a 'rating rule' for the 1931 season which enabled most of the Big Class to keep racing together. This meant that the old yachts were to rate by the Universal Rule, but the rule would only apply to them as regards draught and height of mast. The full clause read as follows: 'If any old yacht built to the 23-Metre or 24-Metre Classes of the IYRU Rule exceeds 76ft, rating (J class) the excess will be doubled. An old yacht not built to the 23-Metre or 24-Metre IYRU Classes or the New York Yacht Club J, K, or L classes, will be allowed a deduction from length in calculating rating of the distance the point of quarter beam length measurement at the bow is abaft a .8 per cent of the LWL from its fore end.'

The effect of this clause was that all the yachts had to make more or less extensive alterations to their spars and sails to conform to the new rule, and this – with the exception of *Lulworth* – they did. *Lulworth* went on the sale list. But no one bought her and she remained in Mr Paton's hands until his death in 1935 when she was converted to an auxiliary ketch.

The rule meant taller masts, though they were restricted by the sail area used, the formula being the square root of the sail area multiplied by 1.7 and adding five to equal the height of the mast. It also meant shorter booms and less sail area. The width of booms was not to exceed 6 per cent of their length, and the depth not more than 4 per cent, and any excess was to be multiplied by the boom length and added to the measurement of the sail area. In other words, there was nothing to prevent the Park Avenue boom being fitted for racing in British waters.

Alterations were also made to the J-Class rules, the main ones being as follows: the minimum weight of masts was set at 5,500 pounds; no standing or running rigging was to be set up or worked below the upper decks with the exception of the fore and head stays; the height of the forestay was not to exceed

Left: White Heather II after her conversion to the rate with J-Class. Her owner, W.F. Stephenson, only sailed her for one season before scrapping her and building *Velsheda*.

$82\frac{1}{2}$ per cent of the height of the masts; and normal cabin fittings became obligatory, and were to weigh not less than seven short tons.

One can see the joint committee's reasoning for these alterations. With the coming of duralumin masts it was essential to specify a minimum weight and one which would en-encourage the building of substantial spars which could stand the strain of the new high aspect sail plan. They also wanted to discourage the all-out racing machine and encourage designs which would have a wider application. But taken together these new modifications sounded the death knell for two fine yachts: *Lulworth*, which could not be altered without enormous expense; and *Enterprise*, which, in Vanderbilt's opinion, was too small to be able to absorb the extra weight involved and still stay the defender of the America's Cup.

The shipyards must have had a busy winter that year and it was King George who gave the lead and the impetus by being the first to announce that *Britannia* was to be altered by Camper and Nicholson's to conform to the new rules. Once it was known that the King was going to continue racing, the owners of *Candida, Astra* and *Shamrock V* quickly followed the Royal lead. The least affected was *Shamrock V*, but the rule covering the height of the forestay meant that she had to have a small bowsprit fitted – not an enhancing feature. She was also given a new metal mast, a great improvement on the wooden one she had used in America. *Britannia*, on the other hand, had to be completely rerigged, which created another wail of protest from

the traditionalists who again bemoaned the passing of the gaff rig on the royal cutter and other yachts. But *Britannia* was to prove herself to be a better boat for the change, even though her sail area was reduced by some 20 per cent. Once her alterations were complete it was decided she should give the other yachts 1.2 seconds per mile. Undoubtedly this was a generous measurement for she now rated at 76.86 feet as against the 76 feet of the others, and she should probably have given more like 7.3 seconds per mile. Her measured sail area was now 8,600sq ft, with the largest mainsail ever made.

Astra and *Candida* were also altered extensively. The keel of both boats was deepened to bring their draughts up to 15 feet, the maximum allowed under the Universal Rule. *Astra* was fitted with a hollow wooden mast and *Candida* with a metal one. *Candida* was also fitted with a small centreplate to counteract the strong weather helm she developed in fresh winds – it was placed well aft and proved very efficient. Although *Shamrock V* had hers removed in mid-season, centreboards from then on were definitely 'in' on both sides of the Atlantic, most of the American M-Class having been fitted with them after *Enterprise*'s victory the previous year.

The new rating meant that at long last the two great yachting nations had agreed on a common formula. At the time it was hailed as an historic step in yachting history and looking back it certainly seems absurd that the only two countries to build and race Big Class yachts should have different rating rules. In a time sense the era of the Js was

Above: Britannia leading *Shamrock V* over the first round of the course on the opening day of the Falmouth Regatta, July 1931./*The Field*

Top left: Charles Nicholson at the helm of *Candida./Beken*

Bottom left: Lulworth by now had retired from the racing scene and had been converted to a ketch. Here she's seen anchored in Cowes Roads, during Cowes Week, 1935. /*Beken*

Shamrock V in a stiff breeze off Cowes, 1931. Notice the short bowsprit, added to comply with the rule that the height of the forestay was not to exceed 82½% of the height of the mast./*Beken*

Above: Candida off Cowes,
1934./*Beken*

woefully short, but neither before nor since has the world seen so many large yachts with the graceful bermudan rigging race together under the same rule.

By the start of the 1931 season the depression was beginning to bite, and there was talk of owners giving up the larger classes. On the cheerful side, however, it was rumoured that the new owner of *Weetamoe*, Frederick Prince, was going to bring the American J across the Atlantic to race against the British yachts.

Neither event materialised, but it was a reduced entry that opened the regatta season at Harwich: only *Shamrock V, Astra* – with her new owner Hugh Paul at the helm – and *Candida* crossed the starting line, Lord Camrose's *Cambria* and Lord Waring's *White Heather II* being laid up. *Shamrock V* – now the only Big Boat racing with a professional skipper at the helm – proved her superiority very early on, and very convincingly. It wasn't until the Ryde regatta in June that her sequence of victories was broken by *Britannia* and, a few days later, by *Candida*. This was a great relief to everyone as it proved that

Lipton's yacht was not invincible, for there was nothing worse for the Big Boats in the eyes of the public than to have one boat always winning.

It was during this series of races that *Britannia* raised for the first time what a yachting correspondent called a 'new fangled' spinnaker 'ornamented with "Mr Tom's Peep Holes"'. Obviously a new kind of perforated spinnaker – 'Annie Oakleys' as the American professional crew called them – had made its appearance in the Solent, and presumably 'Mr Tom' was Tom Ratsey of the sail firm, Ratsey and Lapthorn. It must have done the old yacht some good for she won again some two weeks later at Cowes in only a moderate breeze, and there were increasing comments that she had found a new lease of life. Yachting writers called it a striking tribute to the efficiency of the modern rig. The flaws in it were still to be revealed.

Britannia did not make the passage up to the Clyde that year, or over to Northern Ireland. None of the other Big Boats went either – the expense involved was almost certainly the main reason and, perhaps, inadequate prize money – so there was a large gap in the racing calendar. Both *Astra* and *Candida* used the time to have ballast added, and when racing resumed some three weeks later at Falmouth the share of prizes immediately became more evenly divided. Cowes that year had another week of foul weather and was marred by the drowning of *Britannia*'s second mate who was washed overboard, but *Astra* won no less than five races equalling *Shamrock V*'s number.

The season of 1931 could be called experimental and not only did the Big Class survive but it was proved possible to race successfully under the new rules. *Shamrock V* did not miss one of the thirty-two starts and easily came out top of the class, with eighteen firsts and six seconds. *Britannia* was next with six firsts, four seconds and three thirds, though she only started twenty-one times. *Candida*, with thirty-one starts to her credit, won three, had thirteen seconds and three thirds; while *Astra*, the baby of the class, started thirty times, winning five, coming second in seven and third in two. It had not been a memorable year and is probably best remembered for the Transatlantic Cup being won by *Dorade*, an outstanding ocean racer owned by Olin and Rod Stephens.

On 2nd October, 1931, the grand old man of yachting, Sir Thomas Lipton, died. Apart from the King, Lipton had done more for Big Class yachting than any other man. Single-handed he had fought to recover the America's Cup, and the Americans loved him for it. But in Britain his efforts had been looked down upon by some, especially the Royal Yacht Squadron, which had held out against making him a member till the previous year, a fact that reflects badly on the club not on Lipton.

The squadron's reputation for fustiness and snobbishness was undimmed and an amusing article in an American paper leaves no doubt about the feelings of many Americans, a view shared perhaps by more Englishmen that might be expected: 'It has been said indeed that the best way for an aspirant to crash the club is to disguise himself as an ancient woad-stained Briton and sail past the squadron windows on a skin raft; whereupon the members, enchanted by this glorious survival, would invite him in and make him an honorary member on the spot. Last summer they elected only five members . . . The men of ancestry and spirit who ought to be clamouring at the squadron's doors are either flying or motor boating – and speedboats are one of the things the hard-sailing Squadron abhors.'

Certainly the Prince of Wales followed these modern pursuits with enthusiasm and found his father's yacht a boring place to be.

There's a story (perhaps apocryphal, because no living member of *Britannia*'s crew can recall the incident) that once, when the royal yacht was becalmed, the Prince insisted on standing on the counter in order to drive golf balls into the sea.

Lipton had started negotiations for yet another challenge but then England went off the gold standard and, with the economic situation deteriorating daily, Lipton postponed the challenge. Two weeks later he died.

Shamrock V was bought by T.O.M. Sopwith, a newcomer to the Big Class but an experienced yachtsman (he owned the 12-Metre *Mouette* which he sold to Horace Havemeyer for racing in America). He was one of the new breed of owners, a man who could bring to the sport new techniques based on his own professional abilities as an aeroplane manufacturer.

With *Shamrock V* still on the racing lists and the Big Class enlarged by the conversion of *White Heather II* to race in the J-Class by her new owner, Woolworth chairman W.F. Stephenson, rumours* began to circulate again that *Weetamoe* would be appearing in British waters that summer. It was pointed out that she had been extensively fitted out with a new duralumin mast – which had been stepped $3\frac{1}{2}$ feet further aft than the wooden one – and had other rigging alterations which seemed to indicate that she had been equipped specially to race in British regattas. In particular, she had not been given the fashionable Park Avenue boom and this seemed to lend weight to the rumour that she would be crossing the Atlantic, for although allowed by the new rules its use in British waters was being questioned.

The last time an American yacht had appeared in British waters, one yachting writer noted, had been in 1894, a year of extreme financial depression. It had been exciting and memorable because of the series of matches between *Britannia* and the hitherto unbeaten American yacht, *Vigilant*. Shortly afterwards, the writer pointed out, the country returned to prosperity, and it was to be hoped, he added wistfully, that history

*Stephenson's place in the story of the Js is somewhat anomalous. He was not a yachtsman nor did he ever become sufficiently good to race his yachts himself, and always employed a professional skipper and an owner's representative. Yet he was in the vanguard of supporting the Class, and many a gifted young amateur was indebted to him for giving him the chance to helm a J. He was determined to buy *White Heather II*, not the best buy on the market, because he felt sorry for Lord Waring who had gone bankrupt.

Right: Britannia at the Harwich
Regatta after the conversion to
rate with the J-Class./Beken

would repeat itself. Unfortunately, it did not. *Weetamoe* again did not make an appearance, and the recession deepened.

For the 1932 season the YRA decided to alter the rules again for the old yachts, by giving them a 2½ per cent reduction from their rating. This meant that *Shamrock V*, the scratch boat, would allow *Britannia* 1.8 seconds per mile, and *Astra* and *Candida* 3.6 seconds. This decision, taken after studying the previous season's results, also reflected the YRA's determination to keep the Big Boats racing if they could despite the disastrous economic climate. Along with having *Britannia* racing, the public, owners and crews wanted closely fought contests and prizes evenly divided – and it was up to the YRA to see that they got it. Total dominance by any one yacht spelt disaster and was to be avoided at all costs. No wonder *Britannia*, which by no stretch of the imagination or the rules could have classed a J, had been generously handicapped to allow her to continue racing with some chance of success. To have rated her out of the fleet would have killed the very kind of racing the YRA were doing its best to maintain. Now, recoppered and with a new time allowance, she was about to have one of the best seasons of her career.

By resolution it was also decided to approach the New York Yacht Club 'to consider a suggestion that masts in the J-Class be made of wood or steel whenever racing i.e., whether in American or European waters, also to agree to the minimum mast weights being increased to cover all fittings attached direct to the masts for sails or rigging.'

At that time the minimum weight of 5,500 pounds had applied to the bare mast only and it was interpreted that the YRA's resolution was framed as a move to limit the cost of racing in the Class. As it was, if enough money was expended, considerable weight could be saved aloft through advanced design in metalwork and wire rigging. This was perhaps another example of the British trying to arrest the advance of design, but this time its basis could be said to be economic and pragmatic, not some romantic ideal.

The economic situation being what it was the Big Class again did not go north to the Clyde and Kingstown. But it was announced that *Britannia* would be at the following regattas: Harwich, Southend, Lymington, Bournemouth, Cowes, Weymouth, Babbacombe, Paignton, Brixham, Torbay, Dartmouth, Plymouth and Falmouth, and that, as usual, HMS *Tiverton* would be in attendance. Not a few town councillors must have breathed a sigh of relief when the list was released, because with *Britannia* present the other Big Boats would be with her – and that meant the crowds would be there too to boost the holiday trade.

The regatta circuit had been well established for many years, and was maintained, with the exception of the Clyde, Northern Ireland and Le Havre, through the thirties. There was an almost ceremonial strictness in the order, starting with Harwich, then Southend, Dover, the Solent, the West Country, Plymouth, Falmouth, Fowey, back up to the Solent for Cowes week and then the Ryde and Portsmouth regattas, Lymington, then back down to the West Country for the Torbay regattas at Paignton, Babbacombe and Brixham, and finally Dartmouth. As year after year the Big Boats, along with the smaller classes, appeared at the towns and holiday resorts, so they became to be part of the way of life and the biggest day or week of the summer was when the racing fleet made its appearance.

Each place had its own special flavour and ambience which John Scott Hughes, Yachting correspondent of *The Times*, described so well. There was 'a certain bleakness and inhospitality about the shallow waters of Lowestoft and Harwich; the uneasiness of a berth at Southend, although there the spectator has a better view of yacht-racing than is afforded elsewhere in the world; how Ramsgate always reddens the skin; how at Dover it is always either flat calm or blowing a whole gale; how gladly one always comes into the Solent, but as gladly leaves it, being bound west; how that Paignton is the torridest place in England, whatever the meterological records say; how that Brixham takes the stiffness out of the stand-offish; how the Clyde defies all description, and how precious and dear are its friendships; how it can blow and rain at Kingstown; how exciting, how brilliant, is the muster off Cowes, but how weary one becomes of 'The Week' and the people who come to be seen there, and how Cowes Week seems to exhaust the Solent so that the remaining regattas are a fatigue, so that one the more rejoices to be bound down Channel again, where, at Dartmouth, is held the last regatta of the season, and the loveliest regatta in the world, when the church bells ring all the evening, boys and girls come out in boats and float by singing, and the swans swim delicately in line ahead keeping perfect station; the yachts are "dressed" and fly their winning flags, and, excepting the envious anchor watch, every man-jack is spending money on shore.'

Along with Brooke Heckstall-Smith, John Scott Hughes was the best known British yachting correspondent of his time, and he had the knack of vividly conveying what it must have been like to take part in the

regattas. At the Torbay regattas, for instance, which were festive occasions and none too formal in their approach to racing, he amusingly describes how racing would be conducted from the deck of a Brixham trawler, loaded to the gunwales with the mayor and other local dignatories. Below, in the hold, other guests tucked into the crates of beer and joints of cold meat which had been set up on trestle tables. His description of a start is a real classic being 'conducted in the Devonian language and idiom, but with Latin vivacity. A constant cannonade: "Git ready, *foire!*" But that was a misfire – "'Arry! *Yew fule, yew!* Try t'other . . . Ready? *Foire!*" Smoke now wreathed the trawler, as in some desperate Napoleonic sea-fight; and it is to be feared there were moments when the race officials were hard put to it to keep up with the pace of events. Every five minutes and every ten minutes a class must receive its guns, and at the same intervals its five minute and starting flags. Flags! We were draped, festooned, and garlanded with them; flags of all nations, and the International Code, flags of local and historical significance, and flags of such faded colouring and esoteric design that there could be no knowing whether they had any significance at all. And yet beneath and between all this smother of bunting you might have seen, as I once saw, a deck-chair occupied by an elderly gentleman in a white suit, panama-hatted, working at *The Times* crossword with a gold pencil. The Deputy Lord-Lieutenant, no doubt.'

Early on in the season *Astra* again reduced her sail area, by 200sq ft, to take full advantage of the new regulations, and later *Candida* and *Britannia* followed suit so that by Cowes all three were receiving 7.9 seconds per mile from *Shamrock V* and 2.8 seconds per mile from *White Heather II*.

For once the weather was fine for Cowes Week and *Britannia* showed her form – and the advantages of a good handicap – by winning four firsts and two seconds out of seven starts. After The Week – in which she was third in the King's Cup – *White Heather II* followed the example of the others and reduced her sail area by some 200sq ft so that she rated level with the other 'old' yachts. It only remained for *Shamrock V* to sacrifice some 500sq ft of sail area and there would have been, for the first time in British yachting history, five yachts racing absolutely level. But she didn't, so there wasn't.

In the West Country regattas *Britannia* again did extremely well, gaining two firsts, three seconds and a third from seven starts, which included her 500th race. But her most outstanding race that season was one which she did not even win. She battled for line honours with her old rival *Westward* and

after 50 miles the race ended in a dead heat! A British journalist, Arthur Lamsley, wrote a vivid description of the race from his vantage point aboard *Westward*. 'Pressed by so much sail, we now carried tons of water. Big seas, washing over our bow, rushed along the lee deck up to the companion hatch in a torrent of hissing foam. We were sailing at an angle of 45 degrees! . . . Everyone was drenched to the skin, and it took three men to hold the wheel in the sudden squalls. Her owner became obsessed by the sheer glory of the sport, shouted orders to the crew, and lent a hand at the same time. I watched him kneeling on the lee side of the yacht, peering out towards the open Channel trying to spot the Princess buoy, the sea washing over his legs up to the thighs.'

The 1932 season could be called a year of consolidation for the owners of the Big Boats. Two new entrants to the class, T.O.M. Sopwith and W.F. Stephenson, had been recruited and both had proved themselves worthy members. It was generally accepted that, despite the poor state of the economy, everyone could look forward to seeing the Big Class in 1933 – and they were right.

What no one expected was W.F. Stephenson's announcement at the end of the season that he was going to scrap *White Heather II* and build a new J. Naturally, this news was greeted with delight for here was someone

Right: The opening day of the Royal Yacht Squadron's Regatta at Cowes, 1933. This magnificent aerial photograph shows (left to right) *Astra*, *Velsheda*, and *Britannia* battling it out for line honours. *Velsheda* won./*Murdoch*

Below right: Velsheda's sail plan. /*Camper and Nicholson*

Below: W.F. Stephenson at the helm of *Velsheda*. Daughter Sheila, and teddy bear, stand by./*The Field*

ready to back the class by laying out the not inconsiderable sum needed to build and run a J – and it was being done without any mention of the America's Cup!

Despite the deep depression in other walks of life, the yachting world bottomed out early in 1933 and there were more craft on the builders' stocks at the beginning of the season than there had been for the whole of the previous year. Stephenson, however, did not waste any money and used both the keel and mast of his old yacht for his new creation, which was being designed by Charles Nicholson and built at Camper and Nicholson's. With a new J on the way, it looked as if it was going to be an interesting season but there was great disappointment when it was announced by Herman Andreae that he would not be fitting out *Candida*. However, all the others announced they would be racing.

Astra, once more, was under the captaincy of Ted Heard though it was Paul who would be at the helm; *Britannia*, with her mast shortened by four feet and shifted aft eighteen inches, would be racing; as would *Shamrock V* which was reported to be having slight modifications to her keel and stern. Hugh Paul considered altering *Astra* drastically as it had been suggested that in order to overcome her disadvantage of being so short she

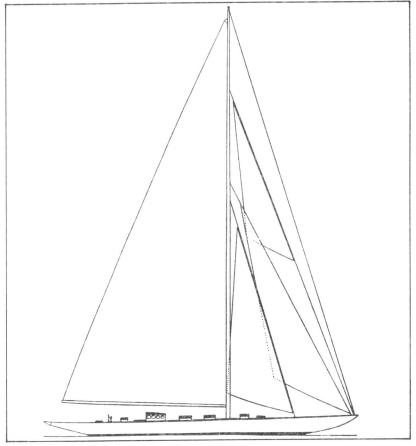

79

should be lengthened by some six feet. Although technically possible the proposal was vetoed by the YRA as being beyond the limit within which an 'old' yacht could be changed and still come under the new rules. The potential cost was not mentioned, but must have been prohibitive.

But all interest really centred on Stephenson's new J, *Velsheda* (the name was a combination of the first two or three letters of Velma, Sheila and Daphne, the names of Stephenson's three daughters) and the yachting press closely followed her construction at Camper and Nicholson's Gosport yard. It was duly noted that she was of all-steel construction – the first yacht to be so built in England since 1913 – had no bowsprit, and, though the Americans were experimenting with double-headsail rigging, was rigged with the traditional triple-headed rig with a boom 63 ft long. This boom was of the bending 'plank-on-edge' type which caused quite a stir when first seen – indeed some people apparently even questioned its legality. It was an interesting arrangement with lateral crosstrees and rigging which could be adjusted so that the boom bent to the natural curve of the mainsail. It seemed as efficient as the American Park Avenue boom, and considerably lighter. However, the design subsequently ran into problems and when it was

adopted by the other Big Boats several yachts suffered broken booms.

As a modern J *Velsheda*'s sail plan was inevitably compared with some of the old 'uns, and it is certainly astounding when reading such comparisons how much sail was crammed on to the old cutters with so little effect, except in a really stiff breeze. For instance, *Velsheda*, 83 feet on the waterline, carried approximately 7,600sq ft of measured sail area while both the 23-Metre *Shamrock* and *White Heather*, 75 feet on the waterline, carried during their classic seasons of 1908 and 1909 not less than 9,000 sq ft with booms over sixteen feet longer than *Velsheda*'s! No wonder so many of the pre-world war one yachts looked like floating laundry lines.

Velsheda was to be skippered and helmed by Fred Mountifield who had been Stephenson's skipper in *White Heather II*. This caused some friendly criticism in American yachting circles from yachtsmen who could not understand why the job had been given to a professional and not to an amateur helmsman. In fact, *Velsheda* often was steered by an amateur but perhaps no one could spare the time to take the J on full time. Very few of the amateurs, the owners included, could afford to ignore their business commitments to be with their yachts all through the regatta season and on passage. Mostly the regattas

Top right: Shamrock V crossing *Velsheda*'s bows, Cowes, 1933. /*Stephenson*

Bottom right: Velsheda off Cowes in light airs. /*Stephenson*

Below: Aboard *Velsheda* during the King's Cup, 1934. W.F. Stephenson (right) keeps a sharp lookout while Captain Mountifield (at the helm) keeps an eye aloft. Despite heavy rain and bad conditions, which prevented the King from racing in *Britannia*, *Westward* won the Cup in about three and a half hours, the fastest time for many years. *Velsheda* was second only two minutes behind./*Central Press*

were arranged round the weekend so that the amateurs could finish work on Thursdays, and perhaps take Mondays off as well. Only the Paul and Davis families actually lived on board their boats throughout the summer, The others had diesel yachts where they slept and ate and entertained their guests. The actual racing, with the owner now an active participant, might have become more democratic but the way of life was still aristocratic and opulent, with everyone changing for dinner.

Britannia, now in her fortieth year, started the season at Harwich as she had left off the previous year, beating *Astra* and the new *Velsheda* into second and third place. Two days later *Velsheda* fared no better and was roundly beaten again by both *Astra* and *Shamrock V*, the winner. In order to get an edge over her new rival, *Shamrock V* had her sail area cut down by some 250sq ft which made her rate 74½ feet compared with the new J's 76. This meant *Velsheda* had to give her 3.6 seconds per mile, *Britannia* 4.8 seconds and *Astra* 5.4 seconds.

However, at Southend *Velsheda* won her first race, with *Shamrock V* coming in a poor fourth, and when, with *Britannia* and *Shamrock V*, *Velsheda* broke the pattern of the last couple of years and went up to the Clyde she won four races in a row, and convincingly.

81

Correspondents started talking about her as a possible challenger for the America's Cup, and by the end of Cowes Week she had won fifteen firsts, seven seconds and two thirds out of thirty-two starts.

Within the context of racing with the Big Class in British waters *Velsheda* could be termed a success. But was she, could she ever have been, a successful challenger for the America's Cup? Hypothetical questions are of course impossible to answer but it must be remembered that *Shamrock V* had undoubtably been much improved since 1930, yet *Velsheda* beat her consistently. That she could have beaten *Whirlwind, Yankee* and *Enterprise* in the light airs that dominated the weather pattern off the New England coast in September does seem at least within the realms of possibility: *Yankee* was best in stiff breezes and had been laid up since 1930; *Whirlwind* was an admitted failure and had not been commissioned after 1930 either; and the successful Cup defender, *Enterprise*, was appreciably smaller than *Velsheda* and would have difficulty in absorbing the extra weight required under the new rules. But it is difficult to see how the Stephenson J could have outsailed *Weetamoe* which, during the three seasons after the Cup races, had kept pace successfully with the new regulations and had been sailed well and consistently, often with Vanderbilt at the wheel.

Whatever might have been the outcome in American waters *Velsheda* was the undoubted champion on the regatta circuit that year, winning twenty races out of forty-three starts, with ten seconds and a third. *Britannia* had another good season, with twelve firsts, nine seconds and three thirds out of thirty-nine starts, and third in points was *Astra*. Amazingly, *Shamrock V* – she had lost her mast during the Babbacombe regatta, the first but not the last J to do so – came a bad fourth with only sixteen flags to her credit out of thirty-four starts.

Babbacombe that year in fact provided the season's most exciting racing, and one of the days which reversed the summer's form where *Velsheda* was able to beat the Royal Yacht in a strong wind. On that particular day a gale was forecast. *Velsheda* took in two reefs and *Shamrock* one, while *Britannia* and *Astra* set a whole mainsail. The course was the usual triangular one, fifteen miles in length, with the yachts going round it three times. Hunloke's article about racing on *Britannia* that day is well worth repeating here in part as it gives the modern reader a vivid description of what it was like to race a J in heavy weather. 'The wind began to blow with very heavy puffs off the cliffs, and just before crossing the line (at the end of the first round) we carried away the clew of our jib.

As Nicholson was then the only designer in the world who had designed two Js it is not unreasonable to have expected him to bring out a radical design. Remembering *Whirlwind*, it was just as well he did not. In fact, *Endeavour*'s hull was quite conventional and was not even tank-tested. Yet, she was possibly the fastest and most beautiful of the Js ever to hit the water. Some say that *Endeavour II* was faster – and indeed she beat her sister ship repeatedly – but the professionals who sailed *Endeavour* across the Atlantic in 1937 say she was not properly tuned that year. And *Endeavour* was the only J ever to beat *Ranger*, the super J.

The new challenger was of steel throughout, with the exception of her decks, joinery work, and rudder. Above the waterline her plates were overlapped, joggled as it was called, but were flush below it. She had a pivoted steel centre-plate, and a circular, electrically welded mast. In 1930 *Shamrock V*, with her inadequate rigging and lack of winches, had been no match for *Enterprise*, 'the mechanical boat' as she had been dubbed. But four years later it was the challenger that possessed every device that human ingenuity and the aircraft industry could produce. She had more winches than *Rainbow* – what is more, they were four-speed ones – against the two-speed winches on the defender. As

well as the normal pedestal winch for trimming the headsails, which was cranked by two or four men, *Endeavour* had ones worked by two horizontal bars which were 'rowed' by two of the crew sitting on deck. With them a two-ton strain could be set up. When hauling in slack the men would be rowing alternatively, but when the load became too great they rowed together.

Another device which the Americans did not have in any form was a wind direction indicator, an invention of Frank Murdoch's. Instead of simply having a racing flag on top of the mast like other yachts, *Endeavour*'s flag was a wind vane which was carried at the top of the mast on ball bearing shafts. The alteration in wind direction moved the flag and this movement was transmitted to a potentiometer. The difference in voltage resistance was followed by a pointer on an eight-inch dial which was mounted on deck in front of the helmsman. By this means the helmsman could follow the exact position of the relative wind.

There was also a wind speed indicator which was specially designed to register low wind speeds. Two wires of equal resistance were balanced in a circuit. One was exposed to the wind and was therefore cooled off in accordance with the amount of wind that passed it; the other one was screened. The

Above: The arrangement for *Endeavour*'s backstay./*Murdoch*

Above left: Endeavour's jam tackle for her main sheet. /*Murdoch*

Far left top: Endeavour's sail plans./*Camper and Nicholson*

Far left centre: These two drawings illustrated well the different lines developed by the two different rules. /*Yachting Monthly*

Far left bottom: Endeavour's removable forestay. When the genoa was to be used it was unhooked and brought back to the mast./*Murdoch*

85

Right: The rowing winches on board *Endeavour.*/*Rosenfeld*

Below: An *Illustrated London News* artist shows how *Endeavour*'s wind speed and direction indicator works, and the mechanics of her Park Avenue boom.

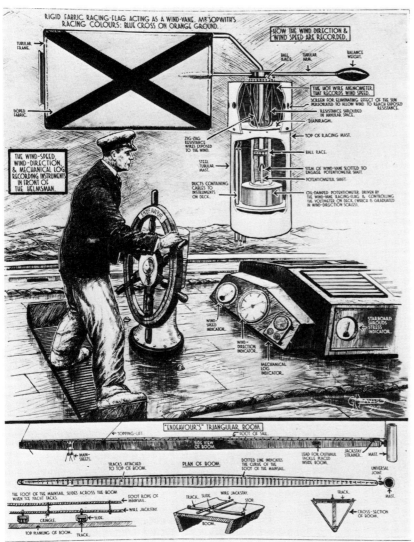

difference was measured and translated into wind speed on another eight-inch dial in front of the helmsman. There was also a seven-inch stopwatch propped against the binnacle which enabled the afterguard to check the time without having to glance down at stopwatches hanging around their necks.

In short, an enormous amount of thought and planning went into the invention and incorporation of these devices, and it is therefore sad to record that many people thought that one of the reasons Sopwith lost the series against *Rainbow*, a slower and inferior boat, was because he relied too much on these devices and not enough on his flair and instinct. The British yacht, a writer in *Rudder* maintained after the challenge, had been handled according to the weight of the wind at the masthead instead of what it was blowing at sea level and this caused the challenger to be sailed at below her maximum potential in light airs. Old Nat Herreshoff's comment was blunt and to the point. 'When is Mr Sopwith going to sail his ship?' he asked.

There were two changes to the rules for the new challenge: challengers no longer had to name their craft ten months before the races, which meant *Endeavour* could be replaced by *Shamrock V* or *Velsheda* should she not prove the fastest of the three British Js. The other alterations stipulated that if one yacht became disabled during a race the other was obliged to finish the course. This last rule was brought in because *Enterprise*, rather absurdly, had been criticised for not retiring when *Shamrock V* had been disabled so that the race could be resailed. This was a sensible innovation as it avoided any recurrence of such criticism – which, in any case, was unjustified as any race is as much a test of a yacht's reliability as it is of her speed and her crew's competence.

The Big Class for the 1934 season consisted of six yachts: *Britannia* was racing again, with a new mainsail and her bulwarks removed; *Candida*, without bulwarks, too, was back again after missing a season; *Astra*, the baby of the class, also with no bulwarks, was still racing under Hugh Paul's flag; *Shamrock V*, now simply called *Shamrock*, had been given a new mast and mainsail and was being raced by her new owner, aeroplane manufacturer Richard Fairey; *Endeavour*; and, of course, *Velsheda*. Occasionally, *Westward* joined in too. All the single stickers were fitted with the new flexible boom, and because the Americans called their boom the Park Avenue, the people at Camper and Nicholson's named theirs the North Circular.

Prompted by the local dignitaries who ran the regattas around the coast, the owners of the Big Boats agreed that year to paint their yachts different colours so that each could be identified more easily by the spectators. *Britannia* remained black while *Endeavour* was painted dark blue, *Astra* turquoise, *Velsheda* white, *Candida* grey, and *Shamrock* what was described as hydrangea blue. This worked well except for *Candida*: Andreae did not like the seagull grey of her hull and had her repainted white.

John Scott Hughes reckoned, some twenty years later, that 1934 was the heyday of the Js in Britain, and another twenty odd years after his remark there is no reason to revise this judgment. The early years were a period of adjustment, 1934 and 1935 were the peak years, but then came a quick and rapid decline. Although Sopwith challenged for the Cup in 1937 there was no Big Boat racing in Britain that year, and there never was to be again.

The 1934 season, however, started as though the Big Boats were going to be around for ever – and that included the remarkable *Britannia* now in her forty-first season. The class even visited Le Havre

Below: The launching of *Endeavour*, April 1934. T.O.M. Sopwith's diesel yacht *Vita* is on the right./*Murdoch*

which they had not done for several years. *Endeavour* and *Velsheda* started as scratch boats, conceding two minutes to *Shamrock* over a forty-mile course; three minutes, twelve seconds to *Britannia*; five minutes, twelve seconds to *Astra* and seven minutes, twelve seconds to *Candida*, which had had her sail area so reduced that she now had 1,430 sq ft less than she had in her first season.

As usual the racing started at Harwich. The regatta was sailed in strong north-easterly winds gusting up to forty knots. *Endeavour* won the first race after *Velsheda*, which had been leading, broke her flexible boom and *Shamrock* had been forced to retire. Then, on the Monday, *Endeavour* won again. Everyone breathed a sigh of relief. At least she was not a failure.

What, however, was showing itself to be a failure was the flexible boom. *Velsheda* had broken one the previous summer, and then another at Harwich; and *Endeavour*'s had snapped during her trials and she had had to race at Harwich with an ordinary boom. 'Again, yachtsmen are asking,' wrote one correspondent of a yachting magazine, 'what is there against the Park Avenue boom? Some say that this flat-topped boom is an American invention, but this is not the case.* Even if it were, this is no argument against

*He was wrong: in the form as it was used on *Enterprise* the boom was conceived by Starling Burgess.

88

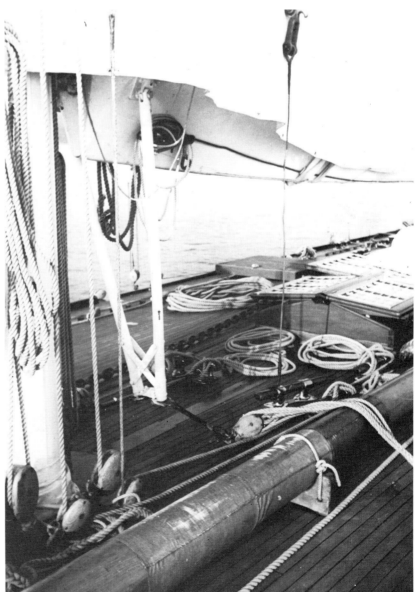

Far left top: Endeavour makes her debut. But the race, part of the Royal Harwich Yacht Club Regatta, had to be abandoned after the first round because of high wind./*Murdoch*

Far left bottom: The control arm of *Endeavour's* Park Avenue boom which controlled the boom's lateral movement./*Murdoch*

Left: A good shot of *Endeavour's* flexible boom. The foresail is being hoisted. The caption on the back of the photograph reads: 'No wonder the boom went!'/*Murdoch*

Below: Endeavour tuning up against *Velsheda* off Cowes. /*Beken*

fitting such a boom to *Endeavour*. Scientifically it is absurd to say that because the Americans first used this boom we should not use it. In the year immediately after the war there were no bermudan mainsails aboard American racing yachts, although such sails were already popular in British waters, but this fact did not prevent American yachtsmen benefiting by British experience. If the Park Avenue boom is the best boom yet produced it should be aboard the Cup challenger, for only the best is good enough for her.'

This is an interesting comment, not so much on the state of play of booms in Britain in 1934, but on prejudice amongst the British yachting fraternity of which the writer was obviously only too well aware. In the event *Endeavour* did fit a Park Avenue boom – only to find on her arrival in America that her rival had fitted an improved version of the type of boom she had just discarded!

Endeavour won four of her five first races on the East Coast and then she had a series of trial races with *Velsheda* in an attempt to copy the Americans' methods of tuning up. However, when reading the reports of these trials, it must be doubted whether *Velsheda* gave the Cup challenger any really professional competition, having, apparently, set the wrong headsails at the beginning of one race and then taking no less than eight minutes to set her spinnaker. But in one trial she must have bothered Sopwith seriously

for he was driven, rather foolishly as it turned out, to break out another of *Endeavour*'s secret weapons, the quadrilateral jib.

For some time Richard Fairey, the owner of *Shamrock* and an expert helmsman having owned the 12-Metre *Flica* for several years, had been experimenting with different combinations of headsails and with new types. He was helped in this by his professional skipper 'Dutch' Diaper, who was a genius at trimming sails, and any new creation would be tested in the wind tunnel at his aircraft factory. One of the new sails he came up with, so it was said, was the quadrilateral jib, which had amongst its several advantages the ability not to backwind a yacht's staysail as its luff was cut parallel to the latter's leach. That is one version of the story.

Uffa Fox, on the other hand, says that the double clewed jib was 'discovered and developed by T.O.M. Sopwith in wind tunnels'.

John Nicholson, however, claims the quadrilateral as his invention. 'We had a

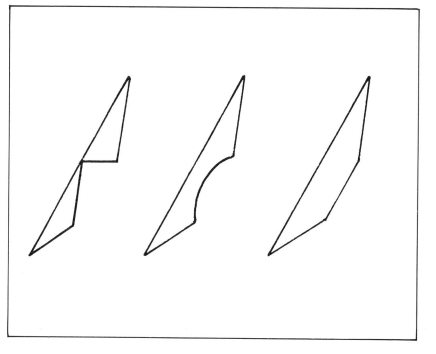

large-scale deck model of *Endeavour* at home in the garden, mounted on trestles which we used for checking sheet leads, etc,' he wrote in his book *Great Years of Yachting*. 'We conceived an unusual headsail which, I am sure, a great many people claim was their invention. The truth is that I had recently been to the Fairey aircraft factory at Hayes where Sir Richard's partner, Mr F. G. Dawson, had shown me their new altitude machine. I was sketching a plan view of this machine's unusual wing with my father, near doodling in fact, and, thinking of the warped wings of the First War Caudron biplane, I added a number of clews to the wing sketch. We then sketched a three-clewed sail and both thought it was worth a trial.

'After obtaining Sir Thomas's approval, we talked it over with Stanley Lapthorn and he, in turn, got in touch with Chris Ratsey at Cowes who always kept his boat *Harrier* in commission all the year round. A triple clewed jib was made to *Harrier* size and in no time we were experimenting off Cowes with Frank Beken taking a number of useful photos. I've always held the view that sail observation is better done off the yacht than on it.

'After pretty exhaustive trials we decided to adopt a double-clewed sail and found that the best method of sheeting was to haul in the lower sheet first and adjust it by the upper sheet. It was so efficient that Frank's (Murdoch) strain gauge registered some extra 2 tons or more on the backstays and the blocks were renewed after the original ones started to split.

'Perhaps we all made a tactical mistake in setting this somewhat revolutionary sail in the Solent, rather than well out in the Channel, as *Rainbow* adopted it in no time.'

Chris Boardman, who was on board *Shamrock* that summer while they were testing the quadrilateral, never heard John Nicholson's name mentioned in connection with this new invention, but as the sail was meant to be a top secret this is perhaps not surprising. Frank Murdoch, who supports John Nicholson's statement, explained how a wind tunnel was used to design *Endeavour* and experiment with idea of a double-clewed jib. A model – $\frac{1}{2}$ inch to a foot – was made and mounted on a swivel so that it could be heeled over at the correct angle to the wind. 'The model had rather a large staysail, and forward of this we hoisted two jibs above each other. The difficulty then was to fill in the gap between them. At first we did not succeed very well, but eventually we were able to close in the whole of the space between the clews; this gave us the double-clewed jib. We then decided to try it full size, which is the only real test.'

Whatever its origins the quadrilateral – or 'Greta Garbo' as the American professionals called it – was a most effective sail, and whoever set it in full view of American spies did Sopwith and his yacht no good service, though of course it would have been impossible to hide once the British yacht had begun tuning up in America.

Of the 12 races she started in before departing for America *Endeavour* won eight and came second in three, and it was generally agreed that she was the fastest and most handsome boat that Nicholson had yet designed. She had been well tuned and the crew had been trained to perfection by Nicholson and Sopwith's professional skipper, George Williams. In fact she had the air of being a winner. There was an aura of success about her which there had not been with *Shamrock V* whose faults many people had been uneasily aware of before she had even crossed the Atlantic. In addition to this feeling of confidence, the British knew that the probable defender had been late in the water and was having a hard struggle to prove herself. Everything, in fact, seemed to be set fair for the blue-hulled beauty.

Yet on the eve of her long voyage to America *Endeavour* was crippled in a manner almost as effective and devastating as the loss of a mast – most of her professional crew walked out over a pay dispute.

The English rate of pay of about £5 a week including racing bonuses was not basically the problem but the amount they were to receive for 'going foreign' and for prize money. Sopwith refused to pay prize money but offered them instead either £6 10s per week if *Endeavour* won and £5 10s a week if she lost, or £8 per week if she won and £4 9s per week if she didn't. This offer was refused, and when Sopwith in turn refused to change his mind thirteen of the crew walked out. (Most of the protagonists are dead now and those alive side with their own: the amateurs with Sopwith, the professionals with the crew, the latter pointing out that all the dissidents immediately found berths elsewhere which would never have happened if their cause had not been just. Certainly, their rates of pay with the built-in prize money looked fairly minimal beside the amounts being earned by their counterparts on the other side of the Atlantic. Then again the dispute may have been only an excuse to bring to the surface basic disagreements between the owner and his crew). Whatever the reason it put Sopwith on the spot as *Endeavour* was due to sail eight days later. It was doubtful if he could have found thirteen professional replacements in the short time available to him, but in the event he did not try. Instead he took on board thirteen amateurs, all with

Top left: Astra leading *Endeavour* during a race in the Falmouth Regatta, 1934. Taken from *Shamrock V* with Captain Diaper at the wheel. /*Boardman*

Bottom left: The evolution of the double-clewed jib.

Above: *Endeavour* tuning up in the Solent. The owner is at the helm./*Murdoch*

dinghy racing experience, and several of these were immediately packed off to gain a few days experience of racing in the other Js which were at Le Havre.

One of them was Beecher Moore who was given a berth in *Shamrock*, and, in an interview in *Yachts and Yachting* (February 1976), he re-captures amusingly and succinctly just what it was like sailing in a J owned by a millionaire aircraft manufacturer. 'We found that when we got on board the boat that it was very much like a well-run country house in that the gentleman does not go into the kitchen and on a well-run J-Class the owner does not go forward of the mast. So while all the theory in the world was at Fairey's fingertips when it came to actually sailing he didn't know that the foresail backed the jib almost all the way round the course.'

The indignation with which the strike was greeted by the yachting press was astonishing and the word 'mutiny' was freely bandied about. One editor of a yachting magazine spelt out exactly what he thought and then went on to castigate the modern yacht hand in general. 'With excellent exceptions, the majority of yacht hands nowadays have become a slovenly and badly spoilt class of men who take no pride in the work or their own vessel's appearance. At almost every popular South Coast yachting centre we have seen large yachts with paid hands lolling about the decks all day, while the topsides obviously need cleaning, or the sails are badly stowed; or the decks go unswabbed morning or evening, and the burgee stick spends the day at right-angles to the mast. One sees yachts in the Solent motoring about with a glorious breeze blowing, while the skipper steers, the owner and his guests look pleasant in chairs, and the crew sit on the foredeck or lean against the mast, smoking cigarettes.

'When crews behave like that it is usually the fault of the owner, who is probably afraid of them or of his ship, and when the skipper is the ruling character aboard and plays for comfort and absence of effort, then the entire crew will become lazy and demoralised.'

Gad, no wonder the country went to the dogs!

This extract, and Beecher Moore's com-ments, was certainly a reminder that though British yachting was becoming more demo-cratic, the British were a long way behind the Americans in their attitudes towards paid hands. In America you were paid for doing the job and were thought none the less of for doing so. But in Britain there lingered the inhibitions and prohibitions of class. A gentle-man did not mix with the professionals, each

had his appointed place, a tacit agreement which suited both parties (photographs of King George hauling in on a sheet were strictly for publicity purposes only). Therefore, young and fit and enthusiastic though the amateurs might have been – and, no doubt, expert helmsmen of their own yachts, indeed one member was an Olympic Gold medallist – could they possibly have been able to adapt themselves to the task of deck hand on something as large as a J with anything like the proficiency of a professional? Frank Murdoch maintains that they took a much more active role in crewing and in fact they devised a new spinnaker drill which proved to be time saving, but when reviewing the story of the fifteenth challenge it is impossible to reach the conclusion that the composition of the crew did not affect the outcome.

But Christopher Boardman, the Olympic Gold medallist and the man who arranged for the amateurs to join Sopwith, feels this is not a fair assessment. He, along with two other young amateurs, had been given a berth for the summer in *Shamrock*, Fairey believing that the talented young should be given the experience of racing a J. (He also probably wanted a trained afterguard for any future America's Cup challenge he might make.)

Sopwith summoned Boardman on board his diesel yacht, *Vara*, explained what had happened and asked Boardman for his help. Boardman gave him a list of names, mostly of members of the Royal Corinthian Yacht Club who he knew might be willing to act as crew members. Sopwith emphasised he only wanted men who'd do what they were told, he didn't want *Endeavour* filled with a crew who kept giving him advice. In the event this is just what he got. But, according to Boardman, the amateurs would probably have been of more help to Sopwith than his afterguard had they been given the chance. The consensus was that *Endeavour*'s afterguard, with the exception of Frank Murdoch, was pretty useless and that the organisation aboard extremely poor.

With *Endeavour* gone the season ended quietly. *Westward* won the King's Cup with a flourish and *Astra* ended the round of regattas at the head of the class with ten wins, ten seconds and four thirds, a really remarkable performance. By contrast both *Velsheda* and *Britannia* performed badly. Again the rumours began to circulate that the King's yacht had been finally outclassed - and this time the rumours proved correct for in the following year *Britannia* did not win a flag all season.

Above: One of the starts during Cowes Week, 1934. First away is *Britannia*, then comes *Astra, Shamrock, Candida,* and *Velsheda.*/*Beken*

The Darling Jade

Am I sentimental about the old Endeavour? *The darling jade nearly broke my heart.*
John Scott Hughes

Wall Street crashed late in 1929 – after the four American Js had started being built. But the sailing fraternity did not really begin to feel the pinch until after the following season when they began to realise that their incomes were going to be very much reduced. George Nichols and Clinton Crane laid up their M-Class sloops, *Carolina* and *Ibis*, and took to sailing the much smaller Fish Class – and enjoyed every minute of it. As Mrs Nichols remarked, 'the new poor must have their amusements.'

The only-relatively-poor, however, kept sailing and nearly all the M-Class owners found enough cash to convert their craft to fit *Enterprise*'s winning characteristics. (The Herreshoff yard was kept busy making Park Avenue booms and shipping them all over the United States, even to South Africa.) *Valiant*, *Prestige* and *Avatar* were all given new metal masts and centreboards. *Weetamoe*, now owned by Frederick Prince, was fitted out to conform with the new J-Class regulations, and raced that summer against both *Resolute* and *Vanitie*. *Resolute* was outclassed but *Vanitie*, owned by Gerard Lambert, gave a good account of herself. *Weetamoe* was sailed a part of the season by Vanderbilt while Lambert, a newcomer to the large class, was given invaluable help by George Nichols and Charles Francis Adams. They had supported him through his first season with *Vanitie* in 1929 but of course had not been available during the challenge season.

Lambert, who had one of the best known professional skippers in American yachting circles, John Christensen, commonly known as 'Cocoanut John', also owned *Atlantic*, the largest schooner in commission on the East Coast of the United States. Both *Atlantic* and her owner* were to become well known to British yachtsmen when he acquired *Yankee*

*He first bid for *Yankee* late in 1932, planning to race in England the following season, and said his offer was the only one he proposed to make. *Yankee*'s Boston syndicate did not believe him and started to haggle. They lost their sale.

after the 1934 challenge and took her to England for the 1935 regatta season.

By 1932 the recession was biting deep into the purses of the American yachting community and, worse, into the very livelihoods of those who depended on yachting to keep them off the dole. Yachtsmen were, not unnaturally, chary about commissioning their yachts. To display such opulence could reasonably be supposed to show, at the very least, a lack of good taste. But the American Federation of Labor appealed, through the columns of the American yachting press, for owners to fit out so that as many men as possible could be given a chance to work in the shipyards. *Weetamoe* and *Vanitie* were fitted out once more, but not *Resolute*. She never raced again.

Weetamoe showed her superiority in any wind over six knots, but the winds proved light that year and in the Marblehead and Newport series of races *Weetamoe* only held *Vanitie* – which had a new mast and double-headed rig designed by Burgess – by three races to two. But she did win the King's Cup for the second year running, though *Vanitie* snatched this prize from her the following year in a summer of even closer racing.

Sailing the J-Class in the United States was a very different affair to the regatta circuit in England. The Cup Defender class boats, as they were commonly called, were just that, and they were built and raced with solely that aim in view. Despite the yacht club cruises, with their famous cups like the King's Cup and the Astor Cup to compete for, there was no tradition of Big Class racing as there was on the other side of the Atlantic. And, with no challenge on the horizon, both amateurs and professionals dispersed the length of the New England coast to race their M-Class sloops, their 12-Metres, and their ocean racers.

Of the four Js specially built to compete for the honour of defending the Cup only *Weetamoe* kept sailing between challenges, and no other J was built as was *Velsheda* in England. For times were hard. There was no tradition to sustain. And no one person, as George V in Britain, had the influence to encourage the enormous outlay needed to run and race such a large yacht as a J. So as

Left: Rainbow leads *Yankee* during one of the Trials to choose the Cup Defender. It was a close-run thing, and many people thought the Boston boat should have been chosen./*Rosenfeld*

Far right: Rainbow's sail plan. / Burgess

Right: Enterprise, the successful Cup Defender in 1930, laid up at Herreshoff's yard./Boardman

Below: Rainbow's lines./Burgess

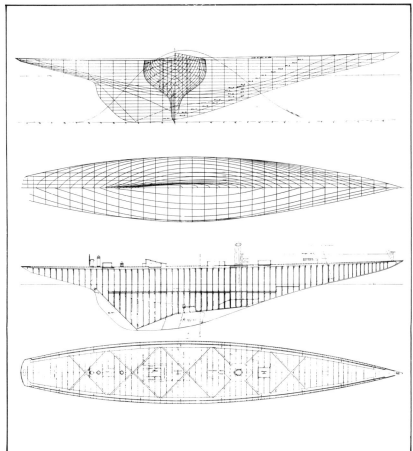

Weetamoe duelled with another Cup defender candidate, *Vanitie*, which was nearly sixteen years her junior, *Enterprise*, *Whirlwind* and *Yankee* lay idle and their designers turned to other less costly projects.

Remembering these three quiet seasons it is not surprising the Americans were slow to take up the next challenge when it came in September 1933 via the Royal Yacht Squadron. However, after some initial hesitation as to who would take up the gauntlet, Vanderbilt decided to build a defender and formed a syndicate which consisted of no less than seventeen people. They named her *Rainbow*, and Starling Burgess was the designer; the builders were – who else? – Herreshoff's. Rather late in starting, the syndicate made up for lost time – or rather had it made for them – because Burgess already had plans for a new J on his drawing board (Lipton's proposed challenge late in 1931 had prompted him to start a new design). These were dug out, overhauled, and approved. *Rainbow* was built in the record time of 100 days.

Although there had been no new J-boats built in America, there had been a great advance in the construction of masts and new rigging methods, along with useful experimentation with sails, winches and mechanical devices. The double-headed rig, first used tentatively by *Whirlwind* in 1930 and then

Rainbow

Fifteenth Defender
of the
America's Cup

DESIGNER: W. Starling Burgess
Burgess and Donaldson

BUILDER: Herreshoff Mfg. Co.
Bristol, R. I.

OWNER: Vanderbilt Syndicate

CLUB: New York Yacht Club

CLASS: "J"—76 foot
Universal Rule

PRINCIPAL DIMENSIONS AND
PARTICULARS

Length overall: 128.56 feet
Length l.w.l.: 82.0 "
Beam, extreme: 21.0 "
Beam, l.w.l.: 20.4 "
Draft: 14.95 "
Overhang for'd: 25.93 "
Overhang aft: 20.63 "
Displacement: 310,812 lbs. (S.W.)
(Inc. rudder)
Sail Area: 7,555 square feet

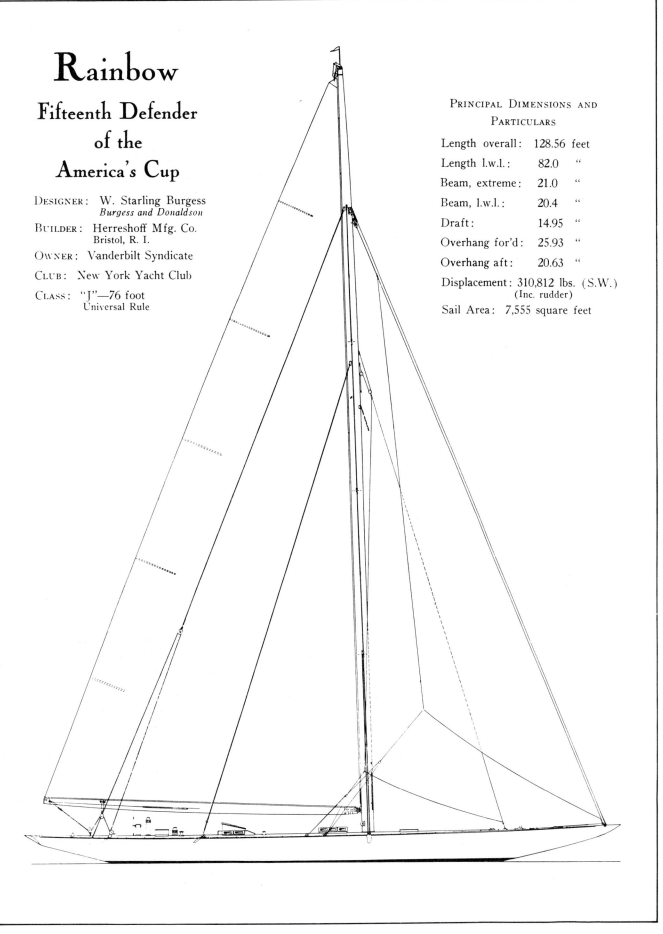

Above: Yankee with her new double-headed rig, 1934./*The Field*

areas of *Enterprise*'s broad V-bow sections which had caused pounding at certain angles of heel. In addition to the extra weight required below decks in the way of accommodation, the new yacht was required to have a heavier mast.

'The design of *Rainbow*'s mast had to meet entirely new conditions,' Burgess commented. 'The weight required by the new rule was so great that it seemed best to build a mast with sufficient fore-and-aft strength to stand unsupported by fore-and-aft staying for the full height of the fore-triangle, this is, some 125ft. Mr Vanderbilt even considered a single working jib to take the place of jib and forestaysail. At any rate, he wanted to be able to carry the genoa jib to windward in far heavier breezes than had been possible with *Enterprise*'s rig. Owing to the great difficulty in handling it, the idea of a single jib on a boom was abandoned, and the working sails were a jib and forestaysail, each with its own pair of backstays.'

Burgess made *Rainbow* 82 feet on the waterline, some two feet longer than his first J. It was, Burgess's brother Charles said quite bluntly in a paper he read the next year to the Society of Naval Architects and Marine Engineers, a mistake. Starling, he said, had not appreciated the tremendous improvement in driving power of the new double-headed rig, and the stability necessary to utilise it. *Rainbow*, he maintained, should have been larger and it was eventually proved that it was beneficial to build to the maximum length the rule allowed – 87 feet.

But in 1934 this principle was very far from being established. In fact, when the record of the other Js was studied, the opposite appeared to be true. *Whirlwind*, the longest of the Js built in 1930, had proved the most disastrous; and *Yankee*, the next longest, had only shown in a strong breeze, not the strength of wind normally expected off Newport in September. It had been the two smallest Js, *Enterprise* and *Weetamoe*, which had been the most successful. And Nicholson, one of the world's top designers, had opted, too, for a moderate length when designing *Shamrock V*.

So, contrary to the accepted generalisation that the longer the boat the faster she would go, it did not appear that anything was to be gained by building a J to the maximum length allowed for the simple reason that the sail area did not increase in proportion to the length of the boat. But there were other, more technical, reasons why the 'greater length means greater speed' formula did not appear to apply to Js and these were ably argued by Professor Kenneth Davidson and his young protégé, Olin Stephens, during a discussion of Burgess's paper.

established by *Vanitie*, was now an accepted sail plan; parachute spinnakers and quadrilateral jibs were cut, hoisted and, eventually, successfully trimmed; bar rigging was introduced.

The change in rules after the 1930 challenge* dictated that Burgess's new design had to be longer so that his new creation could carry the extra weight and still maintain the same power as *Enterprise*. He gave her a longer bow than *Enterprise*, adding more U-shaped sections to take advantage of the change in the rules of the quarter beam length measurement points and to avoid the flat

*'If *Enterprise* had been commissioned this year (1934),' Vanderbilt commented, 'her displacement would have been increased by seven tons of cabin accommodation and by some 1,500lb of mast, an increase of 37% as compared with her 1930 mast. These changes would have decreased her stability, buoyancy, and sea-going qualities to such an extent as (in the opinion of the syndicate) to put her out of the running.'

Above: The foot of *Rainbow*'s mast, showing the winch for the flexible boom. / *Rosenfeld*

The gist of their reasoning was that while a 6-Metre or R-Class boat would, when properly sailed, 'maintain a speed corresponding to the speed-length ratio of roughly 1.2 over a surprisingly range of wind velocities', a J would not. Under the same conditions, they said, its average speed-length ratio was around 1.0, this difference being accounted for by the Js greater speed through water which had the effect of drawing the apparent wind forward to a greater degree than happened in the smaller (and slower) classes. (Uffa Fox has a most effective photograph in his *Second Book* which illustrates beautifully the effect of a J on the direction of the wind, and is captioned: '*Velsheda*'s speed turned the light air over her quarter into a breeze abeam, so that, although she and an 8-Metre were sailing on the same course, she was reaching while the 8-Metre was running'.) A J, therefore, Davidson and Stephens maintained, had to be designed for a lower speed-length ratio than a smaller yacht. They drove home their point of view by means of a graph of hull resistance against speed: three different lengths of J created materially different hull resistances when achieving (at about eleven knots) the optimum speed-length ratio of 1.2, but at the lower speed-length of ratio 1.0 (about nine knots) – the speed attained on average at all points of sailing by the Js in 1930 – the smaller the hull the less the resistance and, therefore, the more efficient the hull.

Why then were Js eventually built to the maximum length allowed? Put simply, they were built to the maximum length to give a more stable base to the vastly improved sails and rigging that were evolved during the thirties. The measured sail area could not be appreciably increased with extra length but the efficiency with which it was deployed could be; and was.

To take the strain of *Rainbow*'s powerful double-headed rig with its sparse standing rigging, Starling Burgess designed a mast which was pear-shaped in section. For the greater part of its length it was eighteen

Above: Rainbow./The Field

Bottom right: Rainbow had beautiful lines, but she was probably slower than the challenger./Beken

inches across and thirty inches fore and aft. This gave it enormous strength but did not help the flow of air over the sail when close-hauled. To enable her to set her huge genoa really flat *Rainbow* was given three sets of spreaders which kept the lateral spread of the bar shrouds within the beam of the yacht.

The bar shrouds gave immense strength – the breaking strain was something like 215,000 pounds to the sq in – and they stretched about $1\frac{1}{4}$ inches per average length of 33 ft, which meant about five inches from deck to masthead when the yacht was close hauled with her lee rail under. In these conditions the mast itself compressed about $1\frac{1}{2}$ inches so it can be seen how impossible it was to keep the mast anything like straight.

No heat-treating furnace could be found to take the required length of rod, so someone had the bright idea of cutting the rods in two and putting the turnbuckle between each piece instead of at deck level.

Another innovation on *Rainbow* was a self-releasing hook at her masthead to receive the headboard of the mainsail so that the mast was relieved of the downward pull of the halyard. This simple device halved the compression strain on the mast, and since the weight of a J's mainsail was in the region of three-quarters of a ton – it can be seen that this was an appreciable lessening of the compression forces at work on the mast when under way. (The challenger too had this

device but it was not automatic and had to be attached by the topmastman when the sail was hoisted.)

Rainbow started the season with *Enterprise*'s Park Avenue boom but it was decided that it was doing her more harm than good because of its weight, and was abandoned. Burgess then designed a 'plank-on-edge' type, which was an improvement on the kind the British had been using – and breaking. Burgess's design was of an advanced nature and was so flexible that in a moderate breeze it conformed on its own to the curve of the foot of the mainsail, while in light weather its horizontal wire trusses could be easily altered by winches. Curiously, *Endeavour*, as recorded previously, started her first season with a 'plank-on-edge' boom but discarded it in favour of a boom of the Park Avenue type. This was slightly different from the kind the Americans had been using in that it swivelled to allow control in the curve of the mainsail.

In hull design defender and challenger were remarkably similar – though *Endeavour*'s longer, more finely drawn counter stern enhanced her beauty compared with her rival. But it was in their masts that the greatest difference in the two yachts' construction was seen. While *Rainbow*'s was pear-shaped and made of riveted duralumin, *Endeavour*'s was a welded steel tube twenty inches in diameter at the base.

Later many people wondered whether

Rainbow's rig had not been too rigid. *Weetamoe*, given an identical mast and staying system by her designer Clinton Crane, may have suffered because of this rigidity and certainly she behaved in a most disappointing way during the Trials. But *Weetamoe* had also been altered radically below the waterline in order to make her less tender and this was probably the cause of her poor performance. When built in 1930 her underwater profile had been almost triangular with the centre of her lead being much higher than the other three Js. For the 1934 season Crane reversed this by dropping the lead two feet and giving her a bulb keel and an entirely new contour. Prince, the only man to own a Cup defender on his own in 1934 and reputed to be one of the richest men in America, asked Richard Boardman to helm *Weetamoe* for the selection trials. Though a crack helmsman in smaller yachts, Boardman was a comparative newcomer to America's Cup racing, and this could also have been a contributing factor to *Weetamoe*'s poor performance.

Weetamoe's crew were the same as in the 1930 season and the afterguard consisted of Spencer Borden, the designer, who acted as 'mast nurse', and two young yachtsmen, Olin and Rod Stephens. Despite this wealth of talent *Weetamoe* would not go. Early on she

beat *Rainbow* but then, early on, so did every other yacht that raced against the eventual defender.

Halfway through the season, in desperation, Crane had *Weetamoe* altered back to her original shape underwater. But still she would not go, and she must have proved a bitter disappointment to her designer and owner. Olin Stephens' comments about her performance were short and to the point. 'It's arguable, but it's generally conceded that in 1930 she was the better boat and *Enterprise*

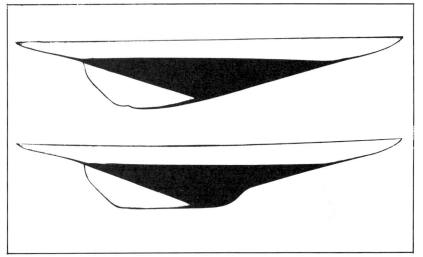

Below: The upper drawing shows *Weetamoe* as originally built; the lower one how she was altered for the 1934 America's Cup Trial races. The changes were a disaster and she was altered back again to her original almost triangular lateral plane. It did no good./ *Yachting Monthly*

was the better organised, especially when *Enterprise* got her new mast. In 1934 *Weetamoe* was altered but the alterations weren't very good and the organisation wasn't very good either. They were very kind to me but really I learnt more about how to do it wrong than how to do it right!'

However, the other 1930 J to join in the 1934 trials, *Yankee*, proved a different proposition. She, too, was altered for the 1934 season but, unlike *Weetamoe*, her alterations proved not only beneficial but positively startling in their effect upon her performance. A heavy weather boat in 1930, which could not be persuaded to move in light airs, she suddenly reversed her form and became a light weather boat without losing any of her swiftness in a breeze. The main alteration was to her bow. This was lengthened and sharpened, the sections from amidships to her bow being changed from U to V-shape. This alteration cancelled the quarter beam penalty she had been carrying which in turn enabled her to carry more sail.

In her day *Yankee* had always been a fast boat – indeed, she held the world record of two hours forty-eight minutes for a thirty-mile triangular course, but she now became, in Vanderbilt's eyes, a frighteningly fast boat in light weather. As with *Weetamoe*, but in reverse, a contributing factor in *Yankee's* success could well have been her skipper, Charles Francis Adams. In 1930, Adams – 'Charley' to his friends – had still been Secretary of the Navy and had not been able to devote his whole time to *Yankee*. But in 1934 he gave the entire summer to the Boston J and there is no doubt he did her a power of good. Ranked by many – including Sherman Hoyt, no mean recommendation – as the best helmsman of his day, Adams had been a yachtsman since boyhood. In 1934 he was sixty-eight, an amazing age still be to racing much less steering a vessel the size of a J. Alongside him on the Boston boat he had two other experts, Chandler Hovey, the manager of the syndicate, and *Yankee's* designer Frank Paine. The navigator was Richard Fay, who the following year raced with Lambert in the British regattas.

Another contributing factor to *Yankee's* improved performance was her superior inventory of canvas. Burrows refused to quote other candidates on making sails and concentrated their entire efforts on making the best for *Yankee* that money could buy. This, plus an outstanding Scandinavian crew under Gust Olsen, made *Yankee* a very formidable opponent for *Rainbow*. During the observation races between June and August she beat the Vanderbilt yacht no less than ten times, a string of successes sufficient to intimidate the most optimistic of men.

Vanderbilt, however, was not only optimistic but determined. He would not give up and it must be supposed that he found some consolation in the fact that *Rainbow* had managed to beat *Weetamoe* five times out of six and *Vanitie*, still not an easy boat to beat, three times out of four. He therefore had *Rainbow* towed up to Newport where he had five tons of ballast put in her. It was, as he admitted, a kill-or-cure remedy, but it worked and in the next two races, the Astor and King's Cups, *Rainbow* won handsomely. Five days later the official trials began and Vanderbilt is on record as saying they were the hardest-fought series in which he had ever competed.

Weetamoe was quickly eliminated after being beaten once by *Yankee* and twice by *Rainbow*, and the honour to defend the Cup became a straight fight between the Boston boat and her newly built New York rival.

Yankee took the first trial race by six minutes and twenty seconds and provoked the comment in the notebook of *Rainbow*'s navigator, Zenas Bliss: 'This will come near finishing our hash.'

Four days later they raced in very light airs and *Rainbow* won by a little over three minutes, then *Yankee* had to retire during the next race after carrying away a jumper strut – and as structural failure was always frowned upon by the selection committee Vanderbilt felt his rival had lost prestige as well as the race. *Rainbow* won the next race as well and her afterguard hoped that that would determine the committee's choice. But it was not

to be and another race was ordered. This was so close that as the two yachts crossed the line no one knew which had won. The spectator fleet did not cheer as they did not know which yacht they were cheering for, and the two yachts sailed on past the line in an eerie silence. *Rainbow*, however, had won by one second, and that evening she was chosen to defend the Cup, a decision which many Bostonians though precipitate to say the least.

Rainbow's rival in the 1934 challenge, *Endeavour*, was undoubtably a remarkable boat, and most contemporary authorities thought her a faster vessel than the defender. She was certainly a very beautiful example of the class with easy lines and a graceful sheer. She was full of gadgets and the latest mechanical devices. Her mast and rigging were equal, if not superior, to *Rainbow*'s – metal rod shrouds had quickly been added to her when it was known that Burgess had fitted them to his design. Her sails were excellent, Sopwith having produced something of a rabbit out of his hat by having the quadrilateral jib. And it was felt by everyone who knew anything about it that here was the most dangerous challenger the Americans had ever had to face.

So why wasn't *Endeavour* successful? Put bluntly it was nothing to do with the boats, but with the men who sailed them. *Rainbow*, probably the slower boat, was better handled, better tuned, and was sailed with more determination and flair than the challenger. This is not to disparage Sopwith's skill as a helmsman – he was brilliant at starting, for

Above: One of *Endeavour*'s amateur crew, Billy de Quincy, holding the spinnaker sheet round one of the preventer winches. Note the rowing bars with which the winches were cranked. /*Boardman*

Left: Charles Francis Adams at the wheel of *Yankee*, 1934./*The Field*

instance, and took the start from Vanderbilt four times out of six races – but there must be a good deal of doubt about his management capabilities. To quarrel with his crew a week before sailing might seem merely inept, but to replace them with gentlemen amateurs, few of whom had ever raced in anything like a J, was surely simply foolishness – or stubborn pride. And the incompetence of his afterguard has already been touched on.

The navigator, for instance, a merchant navy officer called Paul, was really not quite the right man for the job. He was taken on mainly to navigate *Endeavour* safely across the Atlantic and this he did competently. But it was not realised by Sopwith how different were the skills needed by a navigator during America's Cup races, and Paul was neither practised nor quick enough to respond to the challenges of international yacht racing. Apparently, he even had difficulty in calculations before rounding a mark the difference between the real and apparent wind! It seems to be unanimous, too, amongst those who were present, that Gerald Penny, taken on to organise the amateur crew, was superfluous as he had no proper function during racing. It seemed he was only there because he was a fishing friend of the owner. Two other members of the afterguard could also said to be on board because of who they were not because of what they did: Charles Nicholson and Mrs Sopwith. It has been said that Sopwith himself looked upon the challenge more

Far left top: Loading ballast on to *Endeavour*. Later, most of it was taken off again./*Boardman*

Far left bottom: Endeavour under tow at the beginning of her passage./*Boardman*

Left: Out for a practice sail after lunch with the 12,000 sq.ft. spinnaker set. Gerald Penney is at the wheel and T.O.M. Sopwith is on the deckhouse. Carl Hoffenreffer, the manager of Herreshoff's, and M.B. Heckstall-Smith are talking to him while Lady Leon sleeps in the cockpit. /*Boardman*

Below: Ready to go! Mrs Sopwith gives a farewell wave. The gentleman doffing his cap is Charles Nicholson. The owner is at the wheel. /*Rosenfeld*

Above: Rainbow's afterguard: from left to right, Starling Burgess, Zenas Bliss, Harold S. Vanderbilt, Sherman Hoyt and Jack Parkinson./*The Field*

of a personal competition against Vanderbilt than as an international clash between two natior , and this could well account for his rather cavalier attitude.

By contrast, Vanderbilt's team were totally professional and dedicated. Each had his own alloted task which he did supremely well: Bliss, a mathematician, was expert at navigating the kind of courses laid down for an America's Cup race; Hoyt, a brilliant light weather helmsman, was also in charge of sails and was an adviser on tactics; Starling Burgess took care of the mast, rigs and spars; and John Parkinson, the only new member of the afterguard and an ex-member of *Weetamoe*, was relief helmsman.

As in *Enterprise* Vanderbilt steered *Rainbow* on the wind, as well as before the starts and rounding marks. But Hoyt took the helm when the genoa was set and Parkinson usually steered when they were racing off the wind.

It was, in fact, a team effort.

Although Vanderbilt does not say so – he is rather brief about *Rainbow*'s racing career in his book *On the Wind's Highway* and one gets the feeling he was happier not to discuss details – it is difficult to imagine that his organisational ability and enthusiasm was not just as predominant in organising the 1934 defence as it had been four years earlier. His task was not made easier by the fact that there was nothing like the money about as there had been in 1930. *Rainbow* used the same mainsail as *Enterprise* and had, along with other gear, inherited some of the 1930 defender's winches – but the skill and professionalism were still there, and every ounce of it was needed to get *Rainbow* into

first-class trim. As Sherman Hoyt wrote, the tuning-up period was a very harassing time, and nothing could be overlooked. 'For example, blocks of a type that had proved entirely satisfactory on *Weetamoe* and *Enterprise* in 1930, when reinstalled this year on *Weetamore* and *Rainbow* suddenly developed the disconcerting habit of shedding their shells. This was so bad that one of us seriously considered equipping the crew with steel helmets as protection against the chunks of metal that came hurtling down from some hundred feet or more aloft.'

The sails, too, needed close and constant attention and a proper sail log had to be kept, recording the number and length of time set, strength of breeze, performance, and so on, which was a job in itself. 'After a season of looking after the sails of a modern Cup yacht,' Hoyt wrote, 'one longs, with a passionate yearning, for the good old days of one set of working sails supplemented with a couple of light kites. If only there were no more nerve-racking decisions to make – whether to set large ballooner C or genoa D, in combination with small spinnaker B, double-luff spinnaker A or large spinnaker C; or scrap the whole lot in favor of taking a chance with that abomination and dangerous curse of modern large yacht racing, a "parachute" spinnaker. And, when a prayerful decision has been arrived at, frequently it turns out that the sail vital to the desired combination is on the *Bystander*, on *Vara*, stored ashore, or undergoing repairs.'

Hoyt, incidentally, emerges as the hero of the 1934 series. A naval architect by profession he was one of the great yachtsmen of his generation. He might not have had the money or organising ability of Vanderbilt, but his breadth of experience – whether in class racing, team racing, match racing, or ocean racing – was unparalleled. He was also a character, someone everyone liked. He must have been fun to know and to learn from. John Scott Hughes describes him well. 'Sherman is a smallish chap (not the "little runt" he somewhere describes himself), highly charged with some extra special essence of vitality.' In the war Scott Hughes had met General Eisenhower and was struck by the similarity between the two men and called Hoyt a 'pocket-sized sea-going Eisenhower' with the same look of 'amiable belligerency, intense tip-toe alertness, and pervading all the impression of power.' Hoyt obviously did not like the new invention of the sailmakers the 'parachute' spinnaker. Vanderbilt was not keen on it either calling the new device 'extremely temperamental' and requiring 'constant watching and almost constant nursing'. He also added that they were 'rather terrifying to handle in a breeze.' These sails were often over twice the measured sail area of a yacht, and on a J needed at least ten men standing by to handle the sheets and guys.

But gear, rigging and sails apart, the main task was to train the crew and afterguard of thirty to perfection so that each man knew exactly what he had to do and when. It required long hours of drilling and practice, day in day out. As Hoyt put it: 'Sail whenever possible and for as long as possible every day, unless weather conditions or alterations or overhaul at the builders' yard prevent it, and until you get so bored with just sailing around that you long for an excuse for a lay day.' Racing for the America's Cup in the thirties was obviously no more of a glamorous pastime than it is now, and was, with the size of yacht and the amount of money involved, a great deal more worrying.

Vanderbilt must have faced the fifteenth challenge with rather less confidence that the earlier one. He was still troubled with his sail

Below: Endeavour on the slip at Herreshoff's yard being checked by the N.Y.Y.C's official measurer./*Murdoch*

handling, his yacht did not have the normal advantage of being first in the water, and he must have suspected, as many did, that *Endeavour* was fast and her owner no rich amateur dabbler.

After being towed across the Atlantic by Sopwith's yacht, *Vita*, the challenger arrived at Newport late in August in good condition. Sopwith had already arrived and had, at Vanderbilt's invitation, sailed on *Rainbow* during the New York Yacht Club Cruise. From this invitation arose Sopwith's first, but not last, protest when he complained to the New York Yacht Club committee that while *Rainbow* may have followed the new rules to the letter that all Js had to be fitted-out below she had not followed the spirit of them and that, compared with *Endeavour*, she was bare. The result of this complaint was that the committee immediately allowed Sopwith to lighten the challenger below by stripping out certain cabin fittings, including the bath.

Frank Murdoch's comment on this incident is interesting. 'The protest was initiated by Nicholson who later, by agreement stripped *Endeavour* of extra weight below but also went on to reduce the inside ballast progressively during the series with, to my mind, disastrous effect. Her stiffness was being reduced while Vanderbilt put in still more ballast to bring *Rainbow* to her maximum marks. A number of the amateurs were as critical of Nicholson's action as I was but nothing could be done or proved.'

Once *Endeavour* had been rigged for racing Gerard Lambert offered *Vanitie* as a trial horse and this offer was glady accepted. *Vanitie*, which had been rerigged after the 1930 challenge so that she now, strictly speaking, rated at the bottom of the I-Class, was still a very fast yacht, and Lambert was able to hold his own with Sopwith – though doubtless the latter had no intention of revealing his real ability until the Cup races began.

Before embarking on a description of the fifteenth challenge it is worth setting the scene for the series, and to do this through British eyes just as it is intended that in the next chapter the British regatta circuit will be described through mainly American eyes.

Newport is, as the writer J.B. Atkins says in his book *Further Memorials of the Royal Yacht Squadron* very different from any English yachting centre. 'The coast generally is low and is rockbound with rather bare grey shores not much favoured by trees. It is deeply indented and offers a choice of large bodies of sheltered water such as Long Island Sound and Narragansett Bay, as well as a multitude of little creeks and harbours. In most of these there are holiday villages, with houses of the white matchboard type familiar

to film-goers, where visitors and permanent residents sail small one-design classes. Racing mostly take place during the week-ends until the coming of the summer holiday season in July and August. Then there is racing nearly all days for weeks, and apparently heated discussion of rules by the younger and fiercer of the yachtsmen.

'In Long Island Sound itself there are numerous yacht clubs which can be reached easily by motor car or train from New York. The Sound is about a hundred miles long and twenty broad, and would be a quite perfect yachting centre if its breezes were not apt to be very light throughout the summer. For this reason the course for the Cup races was moved in 1930 fifty miles east of the Sound, outside the entrance to Narragansett Bay. Here the yachts race in the open sea, in the best conditions imaginable. There are, of course, occasionally hard winds and calms, but generally the weather cycle seems to be a calm clear night, very light wind till about eleven o'clock in the morning, and then a south-westerly wind which blows at any-thing from five to fifteen miles an hour. About sunset this dies away and another quiet night follows. On most of these good days the sky is cloudless and the sun hot, and only the thinnest clothes are needed.

'To English ideas the absence of any noticeable tide is the chief difference between American and English yachting conditions. Solent tactics, and to a less degree Clyde tactics, are largely determined by the urgent need to avoid foul tides and use fair ones, whereas in America a race is almost a pure test of sailing. The English system certainly has the attraction of giving chances to the less efficient yachtsman; one who has mastered our tide problems is inclined to regard rigging and sail as comparatively easy matters.

To the eastward of the Cup race course lie two magnificent stretches of sailing water each about 25 miles long and 10 wide – Buzzards Bay and Vineyard Haven Sound. Lying side by side, and pointing south-west into the prevailing wind, they both give a lovely beat to windward, ending with a few miles in the open ocean. Here, if the wind is fresh, one meets large, sunlit seas very unlike the short chops of our waters. The sleepy-looking villages of Mattapoisett and Martha's Vineyard are the headquarters of Buzzards Bay and Vineyard Haven yachting, but there are many smaller and just as attractive spots strung out along both waterways.

'The centre of the America's Cup racing is in the fashionable town of Newport, lying by a small, land-locked harbour at the mouth of Narragansett Bay. Many of the old-fashioned big houses are in this small town, but modern tendencies have taken other houses out on to the rocks overlooking the harbour and open sea. As in England, gardening and estate-planning are preoccupations. The grey out-crop of rocks gives a wonderful setting to alpine plants of all sorts and the private landing-places and harbours of the town blaze with colour. The Newport season is a great deal longer than our season at Cowes, as the majority of inhabitants stay there through the hot weather.

'The America's Cup races produce great enthusiasm at the beginning of the series, and many hundreds of vessels of all kinds make the twelve-mile journey to the Cup Race buoy, which lies at the mouth of the bay. The first race usually convinces many of the spectators that a yacht race is a dull spectacle; when they are kept at the 1,000-yard range laid down by the coastguard, they even say that it is intolerable. So the attendance becomes noticeably smaller, and is confined in the end to the enthusiasts in power boats fast enough to keep abreast of the com-petitors. Yet even in the later races the number of enthusiasts returning home and concentrating in the narrow entrance to the bay makes a spirited and dangerous crowd.'

The 1934 challenge was unique. It was the closest Britain ever came to winning back the America's Cup and it was the only time a British yacht had proved herself faster than the American defender on two consecutive occasions.* The other two challenges in the J-boat era were much more relaxed affairs simply because it was obvious the challenger had no hope at all once the first race had been sailed.

But the fifteenth challenge was different for, after the first completed race – an earlier one had been abandoned after the time limit had expired, with *Rainbow* in the lead – it was apparent that *Endeavour* was the faster boat. She won it by 2 minutes, 19 seconds having used her parachute spinnaker to devastating effect. She then won the second race by 51 seconds, and the Americans found themselves in real trouble. *Rainbow*, however, won the third by 3 minutes, 25 seconds after the British yacht had made a tactical error. Vanderbilt then asked Frank Paine, *Yankee*'s designer, to join his afterguard to handle the tricky spinnaker. Paine agreed – and brought *Yankee*'s spinnaker with him. As well as Paine and his sail, Vanderbilt added two tons of lead just as *Endeavour* was having 3,000lbs of hers removed. So far Sopwith had taken each of the three starts but Vanderbilt went over the line first in the fourth race with a lead of 40 seconds which he increased to 1 minute, 15 seconds by the time he had crossed

*In 1920 *Shamrock IV* won the first race because *Resolute* was forced to retire.

Top left: Charles Nicholson and Captain Williams adjusting the stops on the tracks of *Endeavour*'s Park Avenue boom./*Boardman*

Centre left: Endeavour's Park Avenue boom./*Boardman*

Bottom left: When a dispute arose about a difference in interpreting the rules, *Endeavour* was allowed to be stripped below. Here the owner's bath is being removed. /*Boardman*

the finishing line 3 hours, 15 minutes and 38 seconds later. He then added another 1,000lbs of ballast while Sopwith, whose protest at *Rainbow*'s refusal to yield to *Endeavour*'s luff had been refused a hearing by the NYYC race committee, put back what had been taken out of her after the previous race. *Rainbow* then won the fifth race by 4 minutes and 1 second, and the sixth race by 55 seconds. Once more the America's Cup went back into the vaults of Tiffany's on Fifth Avenue.

Described like this, the fifteenth challenge doesn't sound much different from many of the others – before or since. *Rainbow*, once she got going, was the superior boat and the American crew and afterguard were, as usual, better organised and trained than the challenger's mixture of amateurs and professionals. But this summary, though accurate as far as it goes, conceals more than it reveals.

The truth is that the Americans were in dire trouble much of the time and perhaps only won through because of the astute reading of one man's personality by another. But it must be said that much must have been owed to Vanderbilt himself. He had already defended the Cup once before, and with great success. He was the master of one-upmanship – when the Sopwith's asked him to dinner before the series began he forgot to keep the engagement – and he was always willing to take a calculated gamble. William Swan's comment on him was that 'being a brilliant player in any kind of sport or game, indoors or out (Vanderbilt, of course, invented modern contract bridge), Mr Vanderbilt dearly loves to take a chance, with the result that many of his starts are daring and thrilling, and goes on to say that Vanderbilt handled the wheel of his yacht 'as confidently and nonchalantly as that of a motor car.' Sis Hovey (now Mrs Sherman Morss) who often raced against Vanderbilt summed him up as 'a very brilliant, clever guy who would take advantage of you very quickly if he thought he could, but he knew his rules.' He was, in fact, a formidable opponent.

But right from the beginning Vanderbilt and the *Rainbow* syndicate had their difficulties. *Rainbow* was late being launched and there was trouble with the crew over pay. *Rainbow*'s sails were poor and her crew had great difficulty in handling the new 'parachute' spinnaker – the 'Mae West' as the crew called it because of its voluptuous curves. Vanderbilt had a misunderstanding with Burgess and the latter left the afterguard and the designer's job of navigating devolved on Sherman Hoyt in addition to his normal task of being in charge of the headsails. This didn't work out and in fact Hoyt made what he describes as 'an unfortunate guess' during

one race – a rather vital one against *Yankee* which the Boston boat subsequently won. The addition of Zenas Bliss as navigator – on Hoyt's recommendation – followed shortly. Then Burgess returned to the fold to look after the rigging and the adjustment of the flexible boom, his new baby. So in the end the afterguard settled down.

But Vanderbilt also had trouble with his crew. Apart from the pay dispute, which was amicably settled, *Rainbow*'s mate, a man called Klefve, voiced his dissatisfaction with the afterguard when they continually countermanded his orders while *Rainbow*'s bar rigging was being fitted. 'I quit! Let the damned brains-trust do their own work,' he spluttered. A few weeks later he threatened to quit again, this time in the middle of a race. Hoyt accepted his resignation and sent him below to pack. But he was soon on deck again, as he was needed for a vital jibe, and nothing more was said about the matter. The mate's touchiness must have been tolerated by Vanderbilt as Klefve was obviously such a fine seaman. Indeed it was he who guided Vanderbilt from the lee scuppers when Vanderbilt was at the helm and unable to see the set of the sails.

But even when he had settled his afterguard and crew Vanderbilt could not get his new creation to go, and he had the most appalling problem to beat the Boston boat in the official trials. Eventually, he won through and as soon as he was declared to be the official defender once more he was able to practise his renowned ability of getting the best out of both his men and his boat.

In the 1934 series Vanderbilt did not steer the defender to anything like the extent he had in 1930, for it was found that in light weather close-hauled Hoyt was the superior helmsman, especially when the genoa was set. 'I seemed able,' he wrote, 'from the extreme lee side of the wheel in light weather, to see the luff of a headsail and to follow the vagaries of the wind, when there was little feel to the boat.' Vanderbilt, on the other hand, preferred standing upright immediately behind the wheel, and in this position he would act on Klefve's advice. But this was no use in light weather. Vanderbilt, typically, realised this weakness and promptly made it known that Hoyt was to take the helm in the light weather conditions that suited him without having to be asked to do so. To recommend a procedure which meant being relieved of the helm of what, for all intents and purposes, is your own yacht in the middle of an America's Cup race by someone who isn't even in the syndicate really does show what a remarkable man Vanderbilt was. Another example of Vanderbilt's flair for moulding a team regardless of his own personality was when, at the end of the crucial third race, he asked a member of a rival syndicate, Frank Paine, to join *Rainbow*'s afterguard with the specific job of setting and trimming the parachute spinnaker. It says a lot for Paine that he agreed to do so, but it says a lot more for Vanderbilt that he went 'cap in hand', as it were, to a member of the afterguard of a yacht he had only just narrowly defeated to ask his help.

With these two decisions alone Vanderbilt probably ensured that the challenger would return across the Atlantic empty-handed. Certainly his decision to give Hoyt the wheel at a critical point in the third race was the turning point of the series. The challenger was way out ahead and the American yacht's position looked hopeless, and Vanderbilt, along with the Royal Yacht Squadron's representative on board, Sir Ralph Gore, went below. But on this occasion it was not Hoyt's uncanny ability to keep a yacht moving in the lightest of airs that saved the day for the Americans but his astute assessment of his opponent's racing tactics.

Hoyt knew Sopwith well and had sailed with him in England on a number of occasions, and had probably raced against him as well. Anyway, he must have known Sopwith's predilection for covering an opponent even when clearly ahead. In this case Sopwith's lead had been $6\frac{1}{2}$ minutes at the final mark. The wind was very light. In Vanderbilt's words, 'there did not seem to be the slightest chance of catching her,' so he went below to have his lunch, and Hoyt took over.

What Hoyt did, according to his memoirs, was interesting. In order to lure his opponent into tacking, he deliberately pointed higher than he needed to, and well above the course to the finishing line. Sopwith, who could not have been too sure of his relative position to the line, fell for the trick and tacked to cover. 'From being well ahead on our lee bow,' Hoyt wrote, 'he barely crossed us, and without the loss of headway, due to his two extra tacks, it was comparatively easy to pinch *Rainbow* a bit up under his lee bow, backwind him, force him to go about to clear his wind, then ease sheets and resume the course for the finish line of which our navigator, Bliss, had kept me constantly informed.'

Chris Boardman remembers it rather differently. He recalls talking to Hoyt after the race, and Hoyt had said he had simply pointed higher in order to find some wind. Boardman thinks in fact that Sopwith had lost confidence in Paul's navigating and had not been told that he could make the line without altering course.

A spectator on the markboat, *Moran*, saw *Endeavour* sail into a soft spot and then 'with every evidence of panic' come about instead of coming closer to the wind to prevent *Rainbow* getting through. To make matters worse, according to Charles Nicholson who was on board *Endeavour*, the wind veered as Sopwith put the British J about so that when she eventually came round – and it could take a J up to five minutes to tack and gather way again – she was actually heading *away* from the line. Soon Vanderbilt was up on deck again. 'No one moved on board *Rainbow*, no one spoke, everyone was lying flat on deck along the lee rail. Sherman Hoyt, the only one, except the navigator in his cockpit, in an upright position, was sitting on deck on the lee side, one hand on a wheel spoke. The sea was quiet; the little ripples running along the side were quiet; the rig, the sails, the ship, the wind – all was quiet.'

Quiet as they were, they must have found it hard not to cheer out loud when their opponent compounded his error by tacking too late to cover *Rainbow* which promptly sailed through *Endeavour*'s backwind, went on to take the British yacht's own wind and to win by over three minutes, having made up over ten minutes on the last leg. As the American yachtsman Alfred Loomis put it, the race had been given to *Rainbow*, 'wrapped up in cellophane and handed to her on a silver platter with Sopwith's compliments.'

It must have been a bitter blow to the British and a wonderful fillip to the Americans' confidence. If that third race had gone the other way even the determined Vanderbilt admitted the task would have been too much for *Rainbow*. As it was they were only one down with another four to sail.

But it must be said that the first two races were hardly a walkover for the challenger. According to the rules she should have lost the first race before it even began, and she won the second by a mere 55 seconds, after ripping her only – repeat only – light weather genoa* before the start. Luckily, it tore at the clew and held until the last leg of the race when Sopwith was forced to change to a ballooner. It was on this last leg that *Rainbow* gained 40 seconds – or almost half the time she had been behind the challenger at the last mark. If the genoa had had to be lowered earlier the defender must have caught up and overtaken the British J. But then it was a series that was sailed where luck held or failed to, where guesswork worked or not, and where trial and error was the order of the day. Ballast was shifted in and out of both yachts with almost monotonous reg-

---

*Sopwith had borrowed this one from Lambert, after seeing how effectively *Vanitie* had used it. Light weather genoas were hardly used in England at that time.

ularity, *Endeavour* trailed her superior parachute spinnaker in the water as if she was trawling for fish and *Rainbow* couldn't get hers to set properly – and on one occasion nearly lost a race by setting the wrong one. And to cap it all *Rainbow* lost a man overboard in the fifth race and it was only by an extraordinary fluke that he managed to hang on to a trailing line and regain the deck otherwise *Rainbow* would have been forced to retire.

Add to these events the flurry of protests* in the fourth and sixth races which we will discuss in a minute, and it can be seen that the fifteenth challenge was no orderly contest. Nerves must have been stretched to the limit – and tempers.

Endeavour came to the line for the first completed race with the betting odds in her favour but, as Loomis put it, 'with little money in sight'. But there was an enormous waterborne crowd eagerly awaiting the start of the series. They were, perhaps, rather lucky to see anything like a race at all as *Endeavour* was not ready to race at the stipulated time. This was because she had great difficulty in hoisting her mainsail, and the topmastman who had gone up the mast to fix the headboard to the catch was swung against the mast and knocked unconscious.

Seeing what had happened the Race Committee postponed the race 15 minutes in order to avoid a sailover, despite having no power to do so (such a decision could only properly be taken by the representatives of the Royal Yacht Squadron and the America's Cup Committee). However, they said afterwards something had to be done and no one, except perhaps Vanderbilt, objected much. It is

interesting to note, however, that the Race Committee also admitted that had the fault been with the defender they would never have dared to delay the start! Such was the power of the press and the weight of public opinion in America in favour of the challenger. Even Vanderbilt expressed his relief that he hadn't been forced to sail over the course under such conditions, as this would, without doubt, have turned him overnight from being a near-hero to being one of the most unpopular men in America. Sopwith was certainly grateful for the gesture. With his mainsail eventually hoisted he shouted across to the committee boat: 'Thank you very much. They would never have done that in England.'

By the fourth race, however, Vanderbilt was all out to retain the Cup, and the series by this time had developed into a needle match. The start showed this with some tough tactics being used on both sides. The technical side of the incident need not concern us here but it is enough to say that *Rainbow* got the better of the start for the first time in the series, and that Sopwith thought *Endeavour* had been fouled. Vanderbilt, on the other hand, thought *Rainbow* had been fouled. Loomis said that it never occurred to him at the time that either had been, which perhaps underlines his thesis that yacht racing is a matter of opinion rather than of fact. Certainly John Scott Hughes saw nothing, and all the people he asked said they saw nothing either. But it happened right by the committee boat and the committee said later that a foul had occurred. but at the time neither boat raised a protest flag.

Rainbow maintained her lead to the first mark, but just before reaching it found she had been headed by the wind. This, and not the proximity of the challenger, forced her to stand on and then tack. *Endeavour*, on the other hand, had not tacked three miles from the first mark as had the defender but chose to stand on further than was necessary to clear her wind – a tactic she used to good effect, but for no discernible reason, during the whole series. This left her that much to windward of the mark, so that the change of wind was to her advantage. But *Rainbow*'s forced tack destroyed the defender's slim lead and as she went about to go round the mark *Endeavour* slipped inside her, rounding the mark with a 23 second lead. This was the equivalent, at the speed both yachts were travelling, of about one length. *Rainbow*, however, had better way on her and while the British yacht was changing headsails soon began to eat into *Endeavour*'s lead. What happened next is still the most controversial incident to happen during actual racing in the whole history of the America's Cup.

*The protests started, in fact, long before the races even began. Besides Sopwith's complaints that *Rainbow*'s below-deck accommodation was inadequate, one of his afterguard, Charles Nicholson, stated that *Rainbow* was loaded below her marks. A letter by him published in 1935 sets out cogently his reasons for this assertion, and to the modern reader they appear incontrovertible. There can be little doubt that the rules as laid down for the 1934 challenge were inadequately phrased and were interpreted differently by the two sides. This confusion was cleared up the following year after Heckstall-Smith, as secretary of the YRA had reported to the Association that 'The Americans measured the freeboard, or yacht's height, above water, in one way, and we measured it another. The second difference was that the English insisted upon a yacht's immersion marks showing above the water at the time of the race; but the Americans permitted them to be below the water when the yacht was ready for the race with her crew on board.' It was agreed between the NYYC and the YRA that the British should adopt the American method of measuring freeboard while the Americans agreed to accept the British view that the plimsoll marks should show above water.

According to Vanderbilt, *Endeavour* was sailing about two points below the course for the next mark, presumably to facilitate the setting of her genoa.* This completed, she hardened up – in other words, luffed – by about four points, with the defender to windward of her. Vanderbilt did not respond to the luff and, as *Endeavour* bore away to avoid a collision, drew past the challenger and took the winner's lead. Vanderbilt's reason for not responding to the challenger's luff is plainly stated by him: it was not legitimate. If contact had been made with *Rainbow* the challenger would not have hit the American J *forward* of her main rigging, which is what the rules required. Vanderbilt also claimed that according to a film being shot at the time it was quite clear that *Endeavour* ceased to luff when she was still about 90 feet away, far

enough, he maintained, for *Rainbow* to have responded had the luff been deliberate. He speculated that *Endeavour* had borne away early because her owner 'had not had a great deal of experience sailing large yachts at very close quarters.'

Alfred Loomis, who was only half a mile astern of the two yachts at the time of the incident remarked that after *Endeavour* had tacked round the mark she 'bore off so far that she appeared to be heading back for the starting line instead of for the second turn of the triangle' and that when Vanderbilt failed to respond to his luff, Sopwith bore away when the distance had closed to 'perhaps fifty feet'. Scott Hughes makes it sound closer than that: '*Endeavour*'s luff had brought her so close that only a yard of broken water tossed between the two hulls.' He could not have meant literally a yard, but he makes it sound as if it was much closer than Loomis's twenty yards or so, and Chris Boardman on the foredeck of *Endeavour* plainly heard Sherman Hoyt on *Rainbow*'s foredeck shout: 'Luff, Mike, for God's sake luff!' Whatever version one cares to accept, they all sound a lot closer than Vanderbilt's 90 feet, and it is hard to accept his reasoning that he still had time to respond.

Above: Just before the start of of the fourth race. *Endeavour* is in the lead but lost it after an alleged foul which the Race Committee afterwards said was *Endeavour*'s fault. This was taken from the committee boat so they should have been in the position to see what happened./*Murdoch*

*In his analysis of the race Heckstall-Smith (*Yachting World*, October 1934) does not mention *Endeavour*'s reason for bearing away but merely quotes an onlooker's lament that Sopwith had thrown the race away: 'Why did he not check his sheets gently and curve her slowly away and *force* Vanderbilt to go to leeward! *Rainbow* would never have reached through his lee – never – and now look at her, she's out on *Endeavour*'s weather quarter.'

113

One version of what happened next was that, after asking the advice of the NYYC's representative on board, 'Bubbles' Havemeyer, Sopwith did not bother to hoist his protest flag immediately, but deliberately waited until he was approaching the finishing line. Chris Boardman, on the other hand, says that the British afterguard all took so long to make up their minds about what to do that *Endeavour* had almost reached the committee boat by the time they'd decided to hoist a protest flag. Whatever the reason for the delay the result of it not being hoisted immediately was disastrous.

Both yachts had made blunders during the four races that had so far been sailed but it was the Race Committee of the New York Yacht Club which made the biggest mistake of all that day. They refused to entertain Sopwith's protest because he had not hoisted the protest flag immediately as plainly stated in the rules. It was not that the protest – or rather protests, as Sopwith additionally maintained in his written statement that he had also been fouled before the start – was dismissed but simply that the Committee refused to hear them at all. This may seem incomprehensible to the modern racing man, but it must be remembered that there was in those day a tremendous emphasis on gentlemanly conduct and true sportsmanship. Indeed Vanderbilt had been expressly asked by the Race Committee to avoid protesting if he possibly could and they themselves had leant backwards to be fair to the challenger. When Sopwith had complained bitterly about the Americans' different interpretation of the rules on freeboard he had been told he could strip *Endeavour*'s interior completely to compensate for the weight saved by the defender. And, as we have seen, the Committee had delayed the start of the first race quite contrary to the letter of the rules. In short, the Committee must have felt that Sopwith had been given a fair crack of the whip. That he then chose to protest officially not on one but on two counts must have seemed to them to flout the very essence of sporting, friendly competition.

But according to the Committee Sopwith had not only flouted the spirit of the competition but the letter: that at the start of the race it had been Sopwith who had been at fault, and that this foul by *Endeavour* therefore invalidated the second incident. This being so the Race Committee, already painfully aware of the acrimony between the two sides over Sopwith's earlier protests and anxious to avoid any action which might blow up into a row the size of the Dunraven quarrel some forty years earlier, decided to side-step making any public decision at all. The excuse they found was the rule which

Telltale Leaves from an Artist's First-hand Notes at the Cup Races

By COULTON WAUGH

First Race - Endeavour ? where's your spinnaker?

Endeavour's day - Crossing the finish line in the second race -

the final race Rainbow w...

Above: An oft repeated scene, agonizing to *Endeavour*'s well wishers – *Endeavour*, ahead, unable to make her 'Annie Oakley' fill properly./*Yachting*

said any yacht protesting must hoist its protest flag 'promptly'. This, they said, Sopwith had not done. The outcry on both sides of the Atlantic was immediate and immense and the unfortunate Race Committee must have realised they had created just the kind of situation they had been striving to avoid.

From this distance in time, and after reading the contemporary evidence, it is impossible to know the rights and wrongs of the case. There seems little doubt, however, that the Race Committee, from the best of motives, failed to act in the best interests of the sport, and a question mark will now always

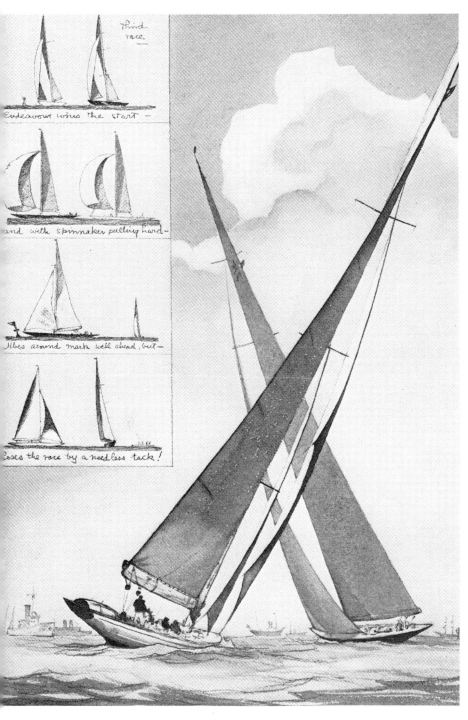

Third race

Endeavour wins the start —

and with spinnaker pulling hard —

Jibes around mark well ahead, but —

loses the race by a needless tack!

Above: Where Sopwith lost the Cup. Leading in the final race, *Endeavour*, still hanging on to her genoa while *Rainbow* carries working headsails, lets the latter split tacks and go off by herself./*Yachting*

vour's owner seemed to lose heart. The fifth race was a convincing win for *Rainbow*. She also won the sixth to give her the series when, amazingly, Sopwith, according to Hoyt, again fell for the latter's trick of luring *Endeavour* into covering when she was ahead and with a clear wind.

The race began with both yachts flying a protest flag over a very similar encounter to the one before the fourth race, but both subsequently withdrew them. *Endeavour* took the lead early on when *Rainbow* set the wrong spinnaker – 'a miserable sail loaned by *Weetamoe*,' as Hoyt described it – and this enabled the British boat, with her large parachute spinnaker drawing beautifully, to draw ahead. 'It looked,' Hoyt wrote, 'all over for us', and Vanderbilt 'highly nervous, suddenly departing from our usual procedure, asked me to relieve Parkinson at the helm and went below leaving me in charge.

'Once again I gambled upon my knowledge of Sopwith's tendency to try and keep an opponent covered regardless of course. Zene Bliss gave me the compass bearing of the finish, then about five miles away. I asked him for the compass course for a point one mile to leeward of the finish, bore off in an attempt to again cut our wind. To do so he had to sail even more by the lee than we had and promptly slowed up. He did not dare jibe in order really to cover us, knowing that we would probably sharpen up and force him to make a second jibe back. We slowly commenced to pull away as he foolishly persisted in his efforts to get our wind which would, due to our sailing by the lee, require him to get on our theoretical lee quarter. He could not do so.'

Rainbow won by less than a minute.

Alfred Loomis thought that by the fifth race it was obvious that Sopwith could not, as he put it, 'be relied upon in the pinches'. His lack of organisation had been against him all the time, as was his luck, his unwillingness to be relieved of the helm, and his lack of experience of racing Cup boats in American waters. Hoyt also picked on Sopwith's reluctance to delegate and commented on the Englishman's 'headstrong and opinionated' manner when he had tried to explain the Americans' method of organising their afterguard. In a sport where one man's assessment of another is normally disguised beneath a mass of superficial compliments, such as opinion is both refreshing and has the ring of truth about it.

Nevertheless, Sopwith was one of the outstanding helmsmen of his day, and he had made far better use of the latest scientific developments and his own professional skill than any other challenger. It just was that the use of them hadn't been quite good enough.

hang over the fifteenth challenge. The only comment that can be made is that perhaps Sopwith should have confined his protest to the luffing incident, which most observers interpreted as being *Rainbow*'s error. Charles Nicholson is on record as saying he thought Sopwith wrong in this respect. '*Endeavour*'s protest at the beginning of the fourth race should certainly never have been made, because, although we decided a definite foul had been made, we did not then intend to protest. Mr Sopwith was urged to do it in indignation at the luffing incident later in that race, and against my advice at the time.'

After the rejection of his protests *Endea-*

The Great Racing Contraptions

We had heard that these great racing contraptions often came into inner harbors and out again and around several times for the amusement of the public, but we could scarcely believe our eyes when we saw them actually do it.

Gerard Lambert

Sopwith returned from America saying he would never race again for the America's Cup unless the rules were changed. Not for the first time the Cup was the cause of acrimony between the two nations' yachtsmen. 'Britannia rules the waves but America waives the rules' may have been merely an American newspaper headline but it was probably very much what the British were thinking too.

Aware of this feeling of animosity and determined to dispel it Gerard Lambert decided to put in another bid for *Yankee* so that he could take her across to Britain the following season which also happened to be King George V's Jubilee year. It was a popular decision which was welcomed on both sides of the Atlantic. This time *Yankee*'s syndicate accepted Lambert's offer. Late in April *Yankee* set sail for England under her jury rig having been fitted out the previous winter with a new interior and new rigging. Frank Paine, her designer, was in charge during the crossing and had with him Alfred Loomis as navigator, John Parkinson and twenty-two Scandinavians under the eye of Gus Olsen. During the crossing she raced against Lambert's magnificent schooner, *Atlantic*, and beat her across by seventeen hours. It was an auspicious start to the most successful season the Js ever had.

The Big Boat class was up to full strength again for the 1935 season and even *Britannia*, now in her forty-second season, had announced she would be racing again. In an attempt

Left: Yankee racing off Cowes. Beyond her is Velsheda./Beken

Summary of the English J-Class Racing 1935

Yacht	June										July							
	1	3	4	6	10	21	22	27	28	29	3	4	11	12	13	29	30	31
Endeavour	1	DNF	1	DNF	..	1	1	1	2	4	4	2	2	1	3	4	1	2
Yankee	—	..	..	1	3	6	5	5	5	1	1	1	7	2	1	1	5	4
Astra	5	2	9	DNF	..	7	Dis	4	1	DNF	2	DNF	4	4	4	2	2	1
Velsheda	2	3	2	2	1	3	6	2	4	DNF	3	3	3	3	2	3	3	3
Candida	4	1	3	..	..	2	2	6	..	2	..	..	1	5	5	5	4	..
Shamrock	3	DNF	..	..	2	5	3	3	3	3	5	DNF	5	7	7	6	DNF	5
Britannia	..	..	..	..	..	4	4	DNF	DNF	DNF	6	DNF	6	6	6	7	DNF	DNF
Westward	..	..	..	..	..	..	..	..	..	..	..	..	..	..	..	DNF	DNF	DNF

	August																			Total Number of Places			
	1	3	5	6	7	8	9	10	12	13	16	19	21	23	24	26	27	28	1st	2nd	3rd	4th	Flags
Endeavour	1	2	1	1	3	3	2	3	2	..	1	2	2	1	4	2	3	3	12	10	6	4	28
Yankee	4	4	4	..	5	2	4	2	1	..	2	3	4	3	DNF	5	1	4	8	4	3	7	14
Astra	2	1	2	3	1	1	5	DNF	3	1	6	5	DNF	2	DNF	1	5	1	8	7	2	5	17
Velsheda	5	3	3	2	DNF	5	6	1	6	—	3	1	1	4	1	6	2	2	5	8	12	2	25
Candida	6	5	6	4	2	DNF	DNF	4	5	..	5	DNF	3	6	3	3	4	..	2	4	4	5	10
Shamrock	3	DNF	5	5	4	4	3	6	4	..	4	4	5	5	2	4	6	5	0	2	7	6	9
Britannia	7	DNF	DNF	..	6	6	7	5	DNF	..	..	..	..	..	..	..	..	..	0	0	0	2	0
Westward	8	..	DNF	DNF	DNF	DNF	1	DNF	DNF	..	..	..	..	..	..	..	..	..	1	0	0	0	1

Explanatory Notes: Although *Westward* was a schooner she raced with the J-boats in the Solent. In the race of August 6th for the King's Cup *Yankee* was not eligible. Due to a series of misunderstandings *Astra* sailed the race of August 13th alone.

to drive her ageing hull through the water at a speed which could even approach the vastly improved Js her copper bottom had been stripped and every conceivable modern gadget added. She now had, in addition to a metal mast, the Park Avenue boom, double-headed rig, bar-rigging and a centreboard. Sadly, it did her no good and she was withdrawn half way through the season without getting a flag.

The other Big Boats were also fitted with the now common double-headed rig, with the fashionable quadrilateral jib, and other minor alterations were carried out to bring the fleet into top racing form. But even as the Js were being given their annual face lift at enormous cost, the first signs of their coming oblivion were being recognised by the very people who raced and built them. During an after-dinner speech Charles Nicholson said that 'with seven J-Class boats racing during the coming season,' he thought it possible 'we were experiencing a boom before a crash,' and added that he thought that leaders of the British yacht racing community were not looking far enough ahead. Richard Fairey, owner of *Shamrock*, on the same occasion expressed the opinion that the Js were too large, too expensive, and not fast enough, and that they were a relic of the past when owners gave their guests hospitality which was beyond the means of any modern yachtsman. The 'Big Boats', he said, should be smaller, and suggested 100 footers, or equivalent to the American K-Class.

In a magazine which was commenting on these pronouncements – under the heading '*Are J-Class vessels too large? – the racing now at its zenith*' – Heckstall-Smith reminded his readers that a J cost £24,000 to build (re-

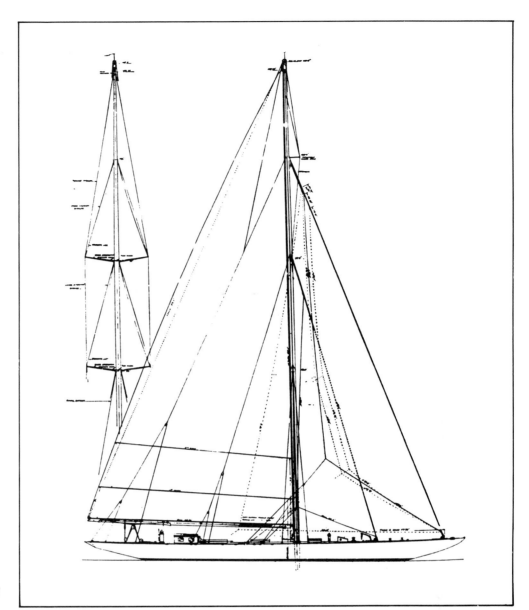

Left: Yankee./*Boston Globe*

Below left: Yankee's crew./*The Field*

Right: Yankee's lines, and her sail plan and new rigging for the 1935 season racing in British water./*Paine*

Below: Three of Yankee's afterguard: Jack Parkinson, Frank Paine (Yankee's designer), and Alfred Loomis./*The Field*

Above: Endeavour being towed in after losing her mast during the Southend Regatta. The same day a man was lost overboard from *Astra* and *Shamrock* broke her boom. *Yankee* won the race./*Central Press*

markably, the same sum it had cost Mr Lee to build *Lulworth* fifteen years before). He cautioned against changing the size of the yachts or the rules, however, holding up the eclipse of the great cutters after 1896 as an example. Then the ruling body had given way disastrously to pressures to alter rules and destroyed a successful fleet of racing yachts. Keep things as they are, was his advice, and the New York Yacht Club seemed to agree with him for, when Fairey issued a challenge at the end of 1935 for yachts of the K-Class to compete for the America's Cup, the challenge was not accepted.

If it had been taken up it is possible that the racing life of the large cutters might have been prolonged beyond 1937. Possible but not likely, and anyway the war would have killed the new class as surely as it irrevocably buried the Js. As it was, criticism of the Js' owners reluctance to sail in winds much over force four first began to appear in the yachting press in England. The amusing *canard* that a J-boat skipper put a lighted candle on the deckhouse before turning in, and if it was alight the next morning there was not enough wind to race and if it had blown out there was too much, was beginning to be widely known if not entirely accepted. These stories all strengthened the argument of those who

had begun to air their doubts about the viability of the Js. But the doubts that had begun to spread about them reflected very well the difference in approach between the British and the Americans. The former wanted yachts they could live on and race in open waters from the Clyde to Le Havre and the East Coast at a reasonable cost; the latter, as always, were primarily interested in out-and-out racing machines which could be used solely for the defence of the America's Cup. That the two attitudes managed to blend so happily under the Universal Rule was nothing short of miraculous. That the rapport did not endure beyond six short years does not detract from the glamour, success and popularity of the class it inspired while it lasted.

Before she left America *Yankee* had been completely refitted. The sparse accommodation had been stripped out and replaced with more luxurious and substantial fittings which were in better keeping with how the British interpreted the J-Class rules on this matter. After all the haggling that had gone on the previous year on this point, Lambert was most insistent that the fittings should follow not only the letter but the spirit of the rule. This was done, and so effectively that when Charles Nicholson first viewed the refurbished *Yankee* at Gosport he turned to

Lambert and said: 'You didn't have to go that far!'

It had also been decided to have a new metal mast, and Paine followed Nicholson's example and made *Yankee* a circular welded one which proved most successful until it was lost during her last race in England. What was more it was considerably less expensive than, say, *Enterprise*'s riveted duralumin stick which four years earlier had cost $30,000. *Yankee*'s cost a mere $4,000.

To cross the Atlantic *Yankee*'s original wooden mast had been cut off just above the jib stay, and a small mizzen was also rigged. The welded mast had been shipped to Camper and Nicholson's yard at Gosport in three pieces where it was reassembled and stepped when the American J arrived in the middle of May.

Unfortunately, there was a delay in fitting out *Yankee* once she had arrived and Lambert thought it better to miss the first regatta of the season, traditionally Harwich, and join the fleet at Southend for her first race, which was on June 6th.

On that day the wind was moderate initially but soon freshened until the fleet were sailing in half a gale. Both *Candida* and *Shamrock*, having heard the weather forecast, had decided not to race at all, perhaps wisely

in view of what subsequently happened. Lambert wanted to start with a whole sail, but was persuaded a reef was in order, and with this he reluctantly agreed. *Endeavour* was first across the line, closely followed by *Velsheda* – which was being sailed all summer by Charles Nicholson – and then *Yankee*. *Astra* was over the line and had to return.

Approaching the second mark, on a broad reach, *Endeavour* still led but *Yankee* had overtaken *Velsheda*. *Astra* was last. *Yankee* decided to jibe at the mark despite seeing that all three British boats had opted against doing so. This proved a wise decision for the British yachts were soon being forced, by the ebbing tide, to sail by the lee in order to try and make the next mark.

By this time the wind had freshened considerably and Lambert was thankful he had taken Frank Paine's advice about taking in a reef, and slowly *Yankee* began to overhaul *Endeavour* as she as well as the other British yachts began to sag badly below the mark. Eventually all three were forced to jibe, and all three came to grief. Sopwith jibed before *Endeavour*'s backstay had been set up properly and her mast snapped forty feet above the deck. *Shamrock*'s flexible boom snapped. Worst of all *Astra*'s steward, while trying to control the spinnaker sheet was catapulted

Above: Yankee close-hauled during her first race at Southend. She won./*The Times*

121

overboard and lost. A boat was lowered, but he was never found. It was a dramatic, and unfortunate, start to the season, but the fact that *Yankee* won the race and still managed to retain her mast gave her crew and afterguard an enormous boost to their confidence.

Minor accidents were not infrequent on the Big Boats but it was rare for so many things to go wrong, and so badly, all at the same time. The previous year *Shamrock* had broken her boom twice, and *Endeavour* once. And some years before a man had been lost off *Britannia*, but otherwise accidents of a serious nature were very rare indeed, and fatalities unknown. This was the first time a J had been dismasted and the cause was human error. The crew member in charge of the windward after runner which was about to become the leeward one was told to cast off perhaps a fraction too soon for there was still some weight from the mainsail on it. As he removed the turns this weight whipped the wire across the deck hitting the crewman in charge of what was about to become the windward preventer stay across the nose. Not unnaturally he let go just as the runner began taking the weight of the mast. This was too much for the runner as it had not yet been belayed, and it slipped off the winch and ran out, and the resulting strain brought the mast down. Frank Murdoch said he had the impression that the mast took a long time to hit the water and that once over the side it was impossible to stand on the deck so that everyone had to crawl round on their hands and knees. The violence of the motion was partly caused by the heavy seas running at the time but also because the centre of gravity of the boat had become so low that *Endeavour*'s deck, instead of tilting, described short violent arcs.

By the next day the weather had deteriorated still further, and racing was cancelled as was the Nore to Dover passage race. By 10th June, however, the weather had moderated and *Yankee* raced against *Shamrock* and *Velsheda* at Dover.

Often it is a visitor who can best spot the idiosyncracies of the host country and Lambert had the ability of describing with warmth and humour the oddities of the English racing scene. 'The race at Dover on 10 June initiated us in the odd method of starting English races, which is so different from the system in this country. Our starting instructions read that when a certain lamp post on the end of a certain breakwater came in line with the east edge of the tower of St Mary's church that we would be on the range, adding as an afterthought that there would be a stake boat a quarter of a mile offshore, but that it had nothing to do with the line. Reading these instructions impressed me with the fact that to succeed in racing in England one must have a knowledge of lamp posts (possibly from nocturnal prowlings) and a thorough familiarity with ecclesiastical architecture.'

Alfred Loomis is equally amusing when describing the racing conditions for spectators at Southend. 'The races start off a steel pier which straddles out into the Thames for over a mile, or until it reaches water deep enough for a boat to float in. The public stands or sits in the draft on the end of the pier, and if a naval vessel isn't located strategically in the line of vision, watches the start. It sees the departing yachts for five minutes or so until they have passed beyond a fleet of laid-up steamships and then after a wait of a couple of hours watches them return. Under normal conditions the racers round the starting boat and disappear from view again to return an hour later and finish the race. Under abnormal conditions such as obtained on 6 June, the wind blows a gale which makes the public blow its nose and wish it hadn't come. The last part of this information I derive from my wife who was scouting English yachting from the pier.'

Mrs Loomis, one feels, did not see British yachting at its best. Nevertheless, it was apparently a memorable sight to see *Endeavour*, with Mrs Sopwith at the wheel, sweep past within a hundred feet of the end of the pier. And, generally speaking, every effort was made by the regatta committees and the owners to arrange courses which enabled the public to see what was going on. In the Solent it was relatively simple as land was never more than a mile away anyway. Southend had its pier. But the West Country regattas had to have special and often very restricted courses to enable the spectators to keep the yachts in sight. This normally meant racing in bays with the start line and the finishing line on a pier or breakwater which gave spectators the best view possible. The courses were laid out so that a single leg was rarely very long – usually about four and a half miles – the complete race being three times round a 12 or 13 mile triangular course. And as it was the contour of the coast that counted in the laying of the courses, not the wind direction, it was by no means always certain that there would be a windward leg.

The regattas were run for every class of yacht, but it was the Big Boats – and particularly *Britannia* – who attracted the crowds. The regattas were usually run by the local yacht club. The entry fees were meant to make up approximately half the value of the cash prizes, the remainder being made up by the town where the regatta was being held. The prizes could be quite substantial and, as mentioned previously, could contribute materially to the running of the yacht if she were really successful. In addition to the cash prize, there was sometimes a cup or some other extra inducement like a bone china tea service. Of course the crew had to be paid their prize money out of the cash prizes – all prize money was paid at the end of the season – but the winner of a race could make quite a substantial profit, especially if the number of entries was large, while the second yacht's net prize money could be quite good, and the third yacht would at least cover her entry fee and expenses.

The races always started at 11am as that was when the public expected them to start. Unlike racing in America, which was run for the benefit of the competitors and no one else, the start was hardly ever postponed. Come squall, rain, fog or calm, the race started, though if there was a real gale blowing the race was simply cancelled. Sometimes there was a time limit, but often the racing instructions simply read, 'A yacht finishing at night will show a "blue light"* when approaching the committee boat and flash her recall number in morse code.' If, however, by 3pm only one round of the course had been completed because of the lack of wind, then the race was awarded to the leader and abandoned. Similarly, if the weather during a race deteriorated badly the race would be abandoned after one circuit and awarded to the leading yacht.

So that the public would know who had won, the winner of a race hoisted a burgee, with her racing flag about ten feet below it. A blue pennant with a white '2' on it and a red pennant with a '3' on it were hoisted in the same manner by the second and third boat. At the end of each regatta every boat displayed the flags she had won and at the end of the season all prize flags, with the yacht's home club burgee, were hoisted, provided, as one of *Yankee*'s afterguard pointed out, 'the boat still had her mast.'

There were other customs that were at variance with established American practice, and they caused some wonderment among *Yankee*'s afterguard. The fact that no prize could be awarded to a yacht until a certificate declaring that the course had been correctly sailed had been signed struck them as odd as they had always regarded their British counterparts as being the epitome of good sportsmen. But they soon saw that it proved an excellent way of settling disputes informally, without an official protest. With seven or eight large yachts manoeuvring to

start in a confined area, technical fouls were inevitable. Mostly these were ignored. Occasionally, however, an owner felt like taking it further. But instead of running up a protest flag, the two owners would get together after the race and sort out the incident with the help, if necessary, of anyone who had witnessed what had happened. When it had been decided who, if anyone, had been responsible the guilty party simply did not sign the necessary declaration and that ended the matter. However, if there was a formal protest it had to be accompanied by a fairly substantial fee, usually £5, and this was forfeited if the protest was judged frivolous.

If the American visitors found some of the British customs confusing, the sailing conditions baffled them completely – at least until about half way through the season. The

Above: A trip round *Yankee* was always popular with holiday-makers during the 1935 season./*from* Yankee in England *by Gerard Lambert*

*This was actually a white flare. It was called a blue light because it came in a blue wrapper.

season of 1935 was one of those British summers where the wind was light and variable much of the time with the occasional hard blow, and it was the fickleness of the breeze, combined with the fierceness of the tides, that *Yankee*'s afterguard found bewildering. Not a day went by without the wind altering two points, and it was not uncommon for it to alter three or four. Sometimes, to their complete bewilderment, it came in from the opposite direction! To open water yachtsmen used to the steady, if light, airs off Newport and elsewhere on the Eastern seaboard the fickleness of the wind was infuriating. Time and again *Yankee* would build up a lead only to have it snatched from her by a shift of wind direction, or a total lack of any wind at all, while any local yacht, knowing the conditions better would be able to make way against the tide by sneaking inshore or by having a skipper who could pick up from a long way off the arrival of a stray puff that enabled the yacht to keep moving. (The Js, once they were moving had tremendous way on them. Reggie Bennett who sailed a lot with Fairey in *Shamrock* remembers how they once won a race when the wind had dropped completely by simply shooting *Shamrock* straight for the line nearly three miles away while her competitors were all over the place trying to pick up a breeze). In one race – mentioned again later – which was sailed in the traditional manner of twice round a triangle, *Yankee* was forced to tack at some point during all six legs and had her spinnaker set on five of them! And at one time five boats, all within half a mile of one another were steering the same course on five different points of sailing.

With these conditions it was obvious that the handicap boats had the advantage provided their owners knew how to manoeuvre them to avoid the soft spots and change their tactics and sails to adjust to the variable wind. *Astra*'s owner was a pastmaster at this kind of sailing, but all the British yachts had had long experience of sailing in such conditions so it is not surprising that *Yankee* did not perform as well as her owner had hoped. But there were other reasons. Her double-headed rig, beautifully adapted for the waters she was accustomed to sail in, was not so good in English conditions where many of her competitors often reverted to the more traditional triple-headed rig to make the best of the light airs when they were on the wind. Another important factor was the placing of her shrouds, which were spaced at a wider interval fore and aft than was customary on British yachts where it was common practice for the shrouds to lead close together abreast of the mast. This enabled them, when running before the wind, to adjust the main

and spinnaker booms more easily, and allowed them to run by the lee much more easily than *Yankee* was able to do. However, when the wind was steady *Yankee* often won, and though this did not prove her to be a heavy weather boat in English conditions it does seem to indicate that her crew could overcome the hazards of the crowded starts and adverse tides when they were not beset by the additional problem of a fluky wind.

On her way round to the Solent from Dover, one of *Yankee*'s turnbuckles snapped. It turned out to be defective, but even so Frank Paine decided to change *Yankee*'s rigging from two spreaders to three, this change having been allowed for when the mast had been built. The alterations were made by the crew as *Yankee* lay off Camper and Nicholson's Gosport yard, and other preparations were made for what was the start of the main part of the regatta season. But her first race in the Solent was rather ignominious as she, along with *Astra*, ran aground. She was soon afloat again but had, of course, lost any chance of winning. In fact she came in well behind *Britannia*. The next day the papers were full of headlines like 'Royal yacht beats *Yankee*' and Hunloke fired

Left: Yankee's runner and preventer winches./Murdoch

Below left: Yankee's main rigging screws./Murdoch

Below: Yankee's runner release hook./Murdoch

off the good news to His Majesty in a telegram and received a warm message of congratulations by return. There was no mention of the fact that *Yankee* had gone aground!

Yankee's next race was hardly more successful and she was not helped by the fact that it was found that in running aground she had jammed her centreboard. The start was complex, the winds were fickle, and the tide was strong, and the Americans must have wondered as Sherman Hoyt did 'how any nation can be so keen about yachting and racing that, in spite of atrocious conditions (in comparison to what we are used to), it had been able to bring all branches of the sport to such a high degree of perfection as the English have done, passes my comprehension.'

After a change of afterguard personnel, made necessary by business and holiday commitments, *Yankee* went down to Fowey in the West Country where she again encountered the multifarious hazards of British yachting. Fowey is a very beautiful harbour, but it is also extremely small. The amazement in Lambert's description of the entire J-Class fleet, two large power yachts, and a host of smaller craft, all anchored within its confines, is barely disguised. Inside the harbour three of the J-Class were tied up alongside one another while outside Richard Fairey's motor yacht *Evadne* almost entirely blocked the entrance. Used to the open waters of Long Island Sound and the spacious harbours and inlets of the Eastern seaboard the Americans found the lack of space in which to manoeuvre their two hundred ton yacht rather unnerving. And when they did get to the start line they fared no better than they had in the Solent and in the light fluky airs that prevailed could only manage a third place.

The fleet then moved on to Falmouth and raced the next day, and again *Yankee* did not show, finishing last. However, the day after, with a steadier wind, she went better and after slipping round *Endeavour* which had hit a soft spot, the American J recorded her second win. From then on, with the newly-joined Richard Fay as navigator to advise him, Lambert began to do better, and indeed *Yankee* won the next two races at Plymouth.* Lambert put it down to the fact that Fay's red yachting pants were lucky, but the more likely reason is that *Yankee*'s crew and Lambert himself were not only settling in to handling the J but had become more accustomed to the conditions and the tactics of her adversaries. There were other factors too. *Yankee* received a new mainsail from Burrows

---

*She was the only J to win three races in a row that summer.

which helped her performance, and during the Plymouth regatta Sopwith was away on business so that the American yacht's main rival was without her best helmsman.

After the Plymouth regatta the fleet moved to Le Havre. It had been the custom in earlier times for the Big Boats to join in the French port's annual regatta but of late this date in the racing calendar had been ignored by the British. Now it was revived especially for the American yacht. Brooke Heckstall-Smith is on record as saying that 'the racing in France is rubbish, but the girls are charming'. Certainly Lambert's amusing account of the proceedings gives the impression that the racing was not taken as seriously as elsewhere. The racing instructions were in French and advised the competitors that the start would be signalled by a blue flag on the yacht club building being hauled down accompanied by a gun though the instructions added, rather confusingly, 'if possible' to this latter signal.

When the yachts came to the line for the first race they saw that the club house, which was almost a mile from the start line, was so bedecked with flags that it was impossible to see any particular one being lowered. *Yankee*'s afterguard decided to rely on the gun and on their stopwatch. This proved to be a mistake as the gun was never fired – or if it was they never heard it – and the club obviously had a different time from that *Yankee* was relying on. Consequently, they started at least five minutes behind everyone else and even when they did manage to catch some of the fleet up the American J was luffed out of the race by *Britannia*.

The next day the Americans carefully checked their stopwatches against the club's chronometer and were glad to hear that after complaints the bunting was to be removed from the club house.

There were two more races at Le Havre and *Yankee* won one and came second in the other. *Endeavour*, however, won the series by one point.

After taking part in the Naval Review on 15th July to celebrate the King's Silver Jubilee, *Yankee*'s next port of call was Bournemouth. But again heavy weather intervened and the regatta was cancelled.* Then came the Ryde regatta on 29th July, and *Yankee* won handsomely. *Endeavour* went over the line too soon and had to return but Lambert timed his start perfectly in a race which included for the first time that season the veteran schooner, *Westward*. *Westward*, however, retired and *Britannia* came a bad last, trailing twenty minutes behind the boat ahead of her. It must have been a sad occasion for many of the old timers who, in an earlier era, had watched these two great yachts battle it out together for line honours.

At the end of this race *Yankee* and *Endeavour* had won six races each, though the British yacht had started in two more races than her rival.

The next day the course was the same but *Yankee* did not fare as well for she ran into the conditions the Americans liked least: light fluky winds and a strong tide. *Yankee* did not make a good start – perhaps the afterguard were still not wholly used to lining up a

*Altogether seven races were cancelled that season because of high winds, and the Js were much criticised for not facing adverse conditions.

Top right: Yankee winning at Plymouth. Hard on her heels is *Velsheda.*/*Yachting*

Centre right: A magnificent aerial photograph taken during the Royal Thames Yacht Club regatta off Ryde in July 1935. Left to right: *Yankee, Shamrock, Velsheda, Astra,* and *Endeavour.*/*Yachting*

Bottom right: Yankee racing in the Solent, in the light winds she had so much trouble with. The photograph shows off *Britannia*'s 'Annie Oakley' to perfection but it is obviously not drawing as well as *Yankee*'s more modern parachute spinnaker./*Beken*

Below: During the 1935 season *Yankee* fought many a close duel with the British boats. Here she is in a fresh breeze nose-to-nose with *Velsheda*. Just ahead is *Endeavour.*/*The Field*

church steeple with a flag pole as a method of starting – but she soon overhauled the rest of the fleet and took a commanding lead of five minutes which she maintained until rounding one of the marks. She then found that the tide was running against her to such an extent that she was forced to kedge, a perfectly standard procedure in British races. However, to the amazement of her afterguard, the British yachts did not follow suit but headed inshore, though in the process they were swept far off course. The Americans stayed put, waiting for a stronger wind, and watched their rivals being swept further and further off course as they crept towards the shore. The wind eventually came but by then the Americans had realised their error. The rest of the fleet, which by this time had managed to get the better of the weaker tide inshore, was well ahead. *Yankee* finished fifth her afterguard in low spirits, and nine races passed before she won again.

The winds were also light and fluky for Cowes Week which followed the Ryde regatta, and in the King's Cup – for which *Yankee* was not eligible to compete as it was restricted to British yachts – the Americans witnessed the kind of start so necessary to make the best of the eccentric weather. The start was with the tide and competitors kedged a short distance up-tide from the line. They then let out about a hundred fathoms of warp which dropped them well below the line. A few minutes before the start, all hands began slowly to haul in on the warp, and then, as the yacht gathered way, more quickly until the kedge came up. By this time they were above the line and had enough way on them to be able to turn and cross

Above: Cowes Week, 1935: *Astra* leads *Yankee*, *Velsheda* and *Britannia* in what looks like developing into a drifting match. *Astra* was at her best in light airs./*Beken*

the start line not too far behind the gun. It amazed them to see a line of yachts, their sails flapping, heading away from the line just as the starting gun was about to go off! Nothing like that could happen back in the dear old USA!

After Cowes Week the next event in the sailing calendar in the Solent before the fleet headed West again was the City of Portsmouth regatta. *Yankee*, having led the whole way won this convincingly though, according to Alfred Loomis, Brooke Heckstall-Smith's account of the race in *Yachting World* was so biased in favour of *Endeavour* that he likened it to a communique from the retreating German army during the last few days of the First World War which read: 'Our storm troops won a glorious victory today advancing backwards seventeen kilometres to a prepared position behind the Hindenburg Line.'

The last race in the Solent took place the next day under the auspices of the Royal Albert Yacht Club – though to call it a race is something of a misnomer. The wind was blowing hard and when Charles Nicholson, the Commodore of the club, casually suggested a postponement this was misinterpreted to mean the race was cancelled, and most of the Js wasted no time in hurrying back to their moorings,* leaving the smallest boat in the

*Reading Lambert's account of the incident – labelled by *The Times* as 'Solent Yacht Race Fiasco' – it does seem that the J-boat owners really were wind shy – not, as we shall see, without good reason.

class, *Astra*, and the American J to their own devices.

Lambert decided it was inappropriate to race because it was quite obvious that *Astra*, while an excellent racer in light airs when she could make the most of her handicap, did not stand a chance against the much larger *Yankee*. However, he decided to show up near the line just to demonstrate he had been ready to race if there had been anyone his size to race against. To his amazement *Astra* not only showed up too but took the gun and started off round the course by herself, completed one circuit before the race was abandoned and then claimed first place and the prize money. Lambert and his afterguard obviously thought that this was a most ungentlemanly way to behave – as did Hunloke who was *Yankee*'s guest that day – but the modern yachtsman would perhaps applaud Hugh Paul's enterprise.

On the way down to the West Country for the Torbay regatta the fleet raced at Weymouth, and *Yankee* came second, beating *Velsheda* by four seconds, *Endeavour* being the winner.

The first race in the series of eight which made up the Torbay regatta was sailed at Babbacombe, and Lambert was horrified to see from the chart that the race seemed to take place practically on the beach. The start line was at an angle of sixty degrees to the first leg with the starting buoy some four hundred yards closer to the first mark than the committee boat which marked the other end of the line. Inevitably, the entire fleet converged on the starting buoy end of the

Above: The caption on the back of this photograph reads: 'Brilliant weather marked the opening today of Torquay Regatta in which all the big yachts, with the exception of *Britannia*, took part. The picture shows *Endeavour* first away at the start.' However, it looks as if *Velsheda* is in the lead though neither her 'quad' or staysail are drawing./*Central Press*

line. Yankee manoeuvred cleverly and crossed the line first, just ahead of *Velsheda*, but the distance between the two yachts was such that 'you could almost walk from the deck of one to the other'. But a cluster of sightseeing craft ruined Lambert's plan and caused him much frustration. The incident was, he said, 'a perfect illustration of the handicaps occasionally suffered in racing in England, not alone by the visitor, but by any one of the boats. It can be argued that such planning distributes the chance of winning – and in fact so it does, by scattering the advantages without respect to your speed. In the races where *Yankee* participated, *Endeavour*, by far the fastest of the English boats, and in my opinion, faster than *Yankee*, only won nine firsts out of thirty-two races.'

In many places the racing conditions did leave a lot to be desired but while they were taken as part and parcel of the regatta season by the British the Americans must have found the happy-go-lucky attitude that prevailed especially in the West Country, rather a strange contrast to their more precise methods of organising races. Sherman Hoyt, who that year was racing in *Shamrock*, recounts how in one race the mark boats seemed to be in the wrong place and foggy weather made it impossible to verify this. 'According to the charted position of the two marks, our speed between them was something like eighteen knots, to windward, with a foul tide and in light weather, but, as we were the only boat that found the marks and won with ease, we made no comment.'

John Scott Hughes also recounts that

during one race on board *Astra* they had been beating up to the mark for some time. It was misty and raining and they were not sure of their position. The day wore on, and they still could not find the mark boat. 'Evening approached. Time had ceased to mean much any more. Suddenly some ears caught the sound of a motor boat, and then, out of the fog, there came our mark boat, *steering for home.* They said they had seen no yachts all day, and were not going to wait any more.'*

Having been baulked by the spectator craft *Yankee* lost out to *Velsheda* and *Endeavour*, and took third place.

Then came the Paignton regatta. This was the first race within Tor Bay itself. The course was rectangular, four miles by two and a half, which had to be sailed round twice. This shape gave the thousands of spectators lining the shore the best opportunity of seeing the Big Boats in action. *Velsheda* won, with *Endeavour* second and *Candida* third, while *Yankee* could manage only a fourth, coming in as much as thirty-three minutes behind the leader.

The Brixham regatta was next. Here, according to Lambert, the Js for once had to take second place in the public's interest as the Brixham trawlers were racing that day too. The winds were light again and *Yankee* came in behind *Endeavour*, with *Velsheda* third. *Astra* finished fourth but with her time allowance took the second prize from the American J by eighteen seconds.

The next day the regatta committee, in honour of the American visitors, arranged a course as similar to that of America's Cup as possible with a windward leg of fifteen miles and a return one sailing before the wind. It was a hospitable gesture which unfortunately went awry as it was the only race of the season from which *Yankee* retired. The wind was light and capricious, and it rained heavily all day, and *Yankee* soon found herself an hour behind the leader. However, she managed to turn the outward mark ahead of *Astra*, but she then saw that the British boat had given up the race and had been taken in tow by the mark boat! This left *Yankee* drifting alone in the rain, and when her tender, *Utilitie*, turned up looking for them Lambert decided to retire rather than be late for a dinner party

*On another occasion Scott Hughes says yachtsmen were entertained by 'the unusual spectacle of a mark-buoy up-anchoring and proceeding to moor in another spot a mile or more away while the race was in progress.'

Above: The Torquay Regatta always included races at Dartmouth. Here the Js can be seen at anchor in the harbour. It can be seen from the crowds how popular they were./*Central Press*

Right: Velsheda hoisting sail while anchored off Dartmouth castle. This shows well how confined were the spaces in which the Js often had to manoeuvre./*Central Press*

which was being given in their honour. Some of the others had given up too but *Velsheda* hung on and eventually won.

The following Monday was the opening day of the Torbay Royal Regatta. Again the winds were very light, and again the Js were beaten by the much smaller *Astra* on handicap. Then, for the first time since they had raced on 4th July, the Americans got a proper breeze and showed their stern to their British rivals, beating *Velsheda* by one minute and 45 seconds, with *Endeavour* third. The course of forty miles was covered by *Yankee* in only three and three-quarter hours.

But the steady wind was not to last and two days later Lambert had what he described as 'a race which in freakishness excelled any race recalled in the history of yacht racing in England among the big boats', and had British yachting columnists backing up his claim. *Endeavour*, hopelessly late, so it seemed, at the start, found a private breeze some time after the start and ran through the entire fleet which, to a boat, had been becalmed. Then, when the wind came, it blew from different directions so that different yachts at the same time, on the same leg and steering the same compass course were both beating and running free. Then, near the finish, a squall close to the shore blew out the genoas of *Endeavour* and *Velsheda* while three hundred yards away *Yankee* lay becalmed. The squall then hit *Astra* and, lee rail under, she headed for the line on a broad reach to win on time-allowance. By this time the Americans had given up taking the racing seriously and were roaring with laughter, and Lambert, who was not a drinker, ordered the cocktail shaker to be brought on deck. The racing was, as he said, nothing to do with foresight or good sailing but entirely how you stood with the Almighty that day.

This was the last race in the Torbay series. *Velsheda* had won three, *Astra* two, and *Endeavour* and *Yankee* one each, and the fleet then moved to Dartmouth for the last two races of the season.

But the light airs the Big Boats had been experiencing for much of the later part of the summer now deserted them and a strong south-westerly got up bringing with it rain and a nasty swell. *Yankee*, as game as ever, raised her racing flag at eight o'clock in the morning knowing she must win both races to beat *Endeavour* in the full series for the season. But it was not until ten o'clock that the others, obviously reluctant to risk their gear, did likewise. *Yankee* left harbour and cruised around with her main well reefed waiting for the others to appear, but the only vessel eventually to appear was the committee boat to tell them that the race had been cancelled, and Lambert was obliged to return to his mooring.

The weather the next day was hardly any better, but this time the committee decided to let the Js race and race they did. Both *Astra* and *Candida* decided the conditions were too much for them. Lambert, who had vowed to win even if he sailed the mast out of *Yankee*, made a brilliant start crossing the line at an incredible ten knots only two seconds after the gun. *Yankee* maintained her lead, and just before the first mark Lambert ordered the double-clewed jib to be broken out. No sooner than this had been done, and *Yankee* had begun to bear away before jibing round the buoy, than a squall hit her. Her mast with a 'grinding, crunching noise such as I have never heard', crumpled and fell over the port quarter. At the time the wind was blowing at about 30mph.

Two of *Yankee*'s crew were thrown overboard, but were quickly recovered, and the British yachts, seeing their visitor dismasted, decided to abandon the race. It was a dramatic end to the finest season of large class yachting the British had ever witnessed.

Below: A dramatic end to an outstanding season. 'Here endeth the 1935 season' was the caption with this photograph from The Field magazine of *Yankee* dismasted during the last race of the season at Dartmouth. / *The Field*

The Super J

My mast is duralumin, but it's costlier than gilt,
The wind that fills my riggin' is a million dollar
breeze.
From my bowsprit to my topsail, I am wholly
Vander-built
And I only go a-sailing in the most exclusive seas.

The nations mourn the income tax, for bread the
countries cry.
But whistle the Endeavour *out, and run the*
pennants up –
Three quarter million dollars will be racing in July
For a mid-Victorian trophy, for a silver-plated
cup.

Redbook, *July 1937*

Before the 1935 season had even finished Sopwith had decided on another challenge for the America's Cup and at the end of August it was announced he would be building a new J, to be called *Endeavour II*, at Camper and Nicholson's to the design, as ever, of Charles Nicholson.*

The news that another J was to be built had a cool reception. With the withdrawal of *Britannia* from racing and the resignation of Sir Philip Hunloke from the Council of the YRA, the yachting community felt an era had ended but were uncertain what would happen next. 'The announcement made in these columns last week,' wrote 'Solent' in *Yachting World*, 'that Mr Sopwith had decided to place an order for another J-Class racer, with a view to challenging for the America's Cup in 1937, was received with mixed feelings. Yachtsmen who favour this big class of beautiful cutters are, of course, delighted at the prospect of yet another ultra-modern boat joining the Class; they also welcome the possibility of *Yankee* remaining here for

*People were beginning to wonder if it was such a good thing that Nicholson should have a monopoly in the design of new Js and with the alterations that went on every season to the existing Big Boats. The fact is that Nicholson and his yard stood head and shoulders above anyone else, and probably nobody regretted not having a rival more than Nicholson himself. Of all the Big Boats, only *Britannia* did not lay up at Camper and Nicholson's but even she had all her alterations made there.

another season. But there is no denying the fact that an equally large if not greater number of yachting folk deplore this class, which has produced such a tall delicate and costly rig that is a source of anxiety in all but the lightest airs. "What fellow in his sense would *choose* a single stick for a 200-tonner, 87 feet on the waterline?" they ask. Admittedly a J-boat can beat *Westward* out of sight to windward, but speed, after all, is only relative, and the old schooner is just as pretty a sight as a J in light airs, while she definitely presents a more thrilling spectacle, heeling over in a blow, than does a bermudan riding to anchor under her bare pole. Such are the opinions expressed.'

The season over Lambert laid up *Yankee* at Camper and Nicholson's Gosport yard and declared he would be racing the following year in England. Fairey announced he would be building a new yacht as well, but a 75 footer to the top of the K-Class called *Windflower*, and Andreae bought *Endeavour* from Sopwith. Soon *Yachting World* was again pronouncing that the Js had outgrown their rig, and that what was needed was a smaller class, like the K, which was more in keeping with the times. Why they – or Fairey – thought a K-Class more appropriate just as the Js had established themselves is hard to fathom. Although smaller than the Js, the Ks weren't that much smaller – about the same size as *Resolute* and *Vanitie* in 1920 i.e. 107 tons and 75 feet on the waterline. However, there was a large difference in measured sail area as a K-Class had only 5,570sq ft while the two American boats in 1920 had over 9,000sq ft of sail. They, of course, were gaff-rigged.

Having announced he was to build a K-Class – and specifying the K-Class as the boat he wanted to sail – Fairey then challenged for the America's Cup, via his club, the Royal London, and the challenge was delivered personally to the New York Yacht Club by Reggie Bennett, one of Fairey's amateur afterguard in *Shamrock*. Change was definitely in the air. But his action, and the feeling that the Js were no longer viable, was attacked by no less a person than Colonel Duncan Neill, Sir Thomas Lipton's representative in

Left: Her rayon quad set *Ranger* 'squats down' and goes for the finishing line./*Rosenfeld*

the *Shamrocks* and a much respected elder statesman in the yachting community. The Js, Neill said, were in existence, were successful – and certainly no more prone to losing spars than the earlier Big Boats had been – and the cause of the Big Boat class would not be furthered by the appearance in their midst of a racer built to a different rating. In short, Fairey's sponsorship of the K-Class would not be welcomed.

In addition Neill made it plain that he thought Fairey had jumped the gun by issuing his challenge. 'In my opinion it is a pity that the Royal London YC sent a challenge to the NYYC (as I have heard) on behalf of Commodore Fairey with a K-Class vessel, seeing that they must have known that Mr Sopwith was building a new J-Class cutter with a view to challenging through his club in 1936, not as "Solent" thinks, in 1937. There is an unwritten custom that a defeated owner in a cup challenger should have the first chance of getting his revenge.'

Frank Murdoch weighed in on the side of Duncan Neill when he pointed out that a K-Class Yacht would be no more free from breakdown in rig than would a J – one of the main reasons why the yachting press was supporting the introduction of the K. 'The required strength of the mast of a J-Class Yacht,' he wrote, 'is not arrived at by calculation of the loads involved, as in any other engineering problem, but by building the strongest mast possible at the minimum weight allowed by the rule. This weight is a function of the sail area, and, though adequate when decided upon for boats of the *Shamrock* and *Enterprise* types, it is no longer quite sufficient for the more powerful and heavier hulls now being built to the J-Class. There is little reason to think that the K-Class will have less trouble in this direction as long as the rule remains as it is and stability and displacement are not taken into account in the mast weight.' Anyway, Murdoch pointed out, if *Windflower* were built, she would have no trial horse to race against.

Opinion, however, was fairly divided on Fairey's right to challenge and on the class he had chosen. It had been public knowledge since before the 1934 challenge that he was intending to try and win back the Cup if Sopwith failed – and even in those early days it was known that he was not satisfied that the future of the Big Class lay with the Js. Times had changed as quickly as had the methods of building a large racing yacht and Fairey was in the forefront of trying to get the yachting fraternity to realise this. But as it turned out his enthusiasm for change was wasted.

The New York Yacht Club soon made it known that they preferred 'yachts of the largest and fastest class racing at the time and eligible under the deed of gift' and that they also thought that 'in the highly unsettled state of the world political and economic situation' it was not the time to start a new class even though it might be less expensive than the existing J-Class. The challenge was not exactly turned down – everyone was much too polite for that – but it wasn't exactly met with open arms. Fairey took the hint and withdrew. If he had challenged with a J-Class boat the NYYC would have been bound to take it up, if only because they had never previously turned a challenge down. By stipulating a new class of boat, however, he made it a challenge with special conditions attached and this meant the NYYC were not bound to accept it. This left the field open to Sopwith. But before he could do anything officially he was warned off by a senior member of the NYYC who told him a challenge would not be welcome in 1936 because it was Presidential election year.

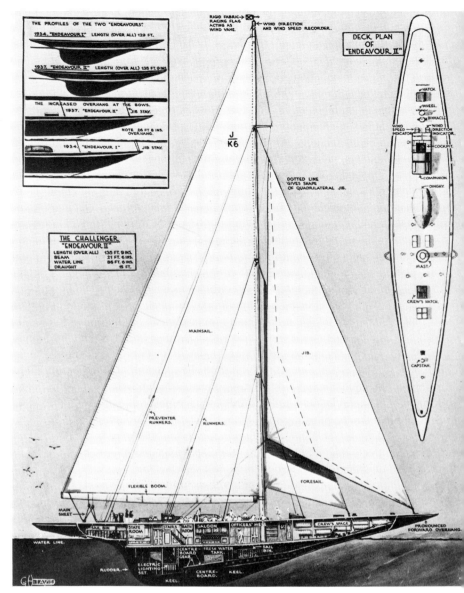

Above: An *Illustrated London News* artist shows the magazine's readers the intricacies of the Challenger. /*Illustrated London News*

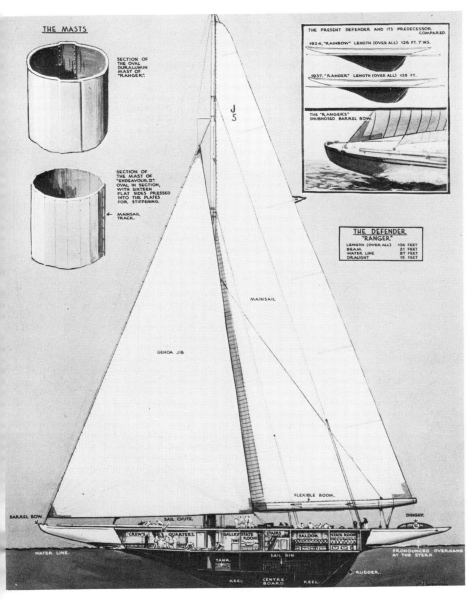

THE MASTS

SECTION OF THE OVAL DURALUMIN MAST OF "RANGER".

SECTION OF THE MAST OF "ENDEAVOUR II" OVAL IN SECTION, WITH SIXTEEN FLAT SIDES PRESSED INTO THE PLATES FOR STIFFENING.

MAINSAIL TRACK.

J 5

THE PRESENT DEFENDER AND ITS PREDECESSOR COMPARED.
1934. "RAINBOW" LENGTH (OVER ALL) 126 FT. 7 INS.
1937. "RANGER" LENGTH (OVER ALL) 135 FT.

THE "RANGER'S" SNUBNOSED BARREL BOW.

THE DEFENDER 'RANGER'

LENGTH (OVER ALL)	135 FEET
BEAM	21 FEET
WATER LINE	87 FEET
DRAUGHT	15 FEET

MAINSAIL

GENOA JIB

FLEXIBLE BOOM.

BARREL BOW.
SAIL CHUTE.
CREW'S QUARTERS.
GALLEY
STATE ROOM
STAIRS
SALOON.
STATE ROOM
DINGHY.
PRONOUNCED OVERHANG AT THE STERN.
WATER LINE.
TANK.
SAIL BIN.
KEEL.
CENTRE BOARD.
KEEL.
RUDDER.

Above: and the Defender.
/*Illustrated London News*

The decision to build *Endeavour II* to the greatest length allowed by the rules – 87 feet – was taken after considering *Yankee's* performance of the season just ended. It had also become increasingly obvious to everyone that the new headsails that had been developed, including the parachute spinnaker and the quadrilateral, had made it imperative that a hull of sufficient power and stability be developed to carry them. Like *Endeavour*, the new potential challenger was of all-steel construction but with flush-plating above water level as well as below. The extra length and weight, some twenty tons, made her look enormous in the Camper and Nicholson building shed. On first seeing her, Sopwith exclaimed to her designer, 'Good Lord, Charlie, she's like a ruddy great pantechnicon.'

In January 1936 King George V died, sealing the fate of *Britannia* and finishing a great era in yachting history. No one knew what was going to happen next but everyone felt that nothing would ever be the same again. It wasn't.

For a short time it was rumoured that *Britannia* would be commissioned for the 1936 season. This was probably wishful thinking and the other rumour, that the Royal yacht was to be sold, was probably closer to the new King's thinking. However, it was eventually decided to strip *Britannia* and sell off her gear, and then sink the hull. At the end of June all her spars and gear was auctioned off. Andreae had already purchased her Park Avenue boom for *Endeavour*, but the rest went to souvenir hunters and a smattering of genuine yachtsmen. Her mainmast went for £80, her port and starboard lights for £32 10s 'after some keen bidding' and her foresails fetched from between £1 and £4. Then, a matter of weeks later, she was towed out to sea off St Catherine's Point on the Isle of Wight and scuttled. It now seems a barbarous act for she was a unique vessel and still in perfect racing trim. Many sentimental lines were written about the appropriateness of her end, but there were many others who thought it was a waste of a beautiful yacht. But their suggestions to use her as a training vessel were not heeded and the explosives on board her were detonated and she went to the bottom.

With the death of the King and the end of *Britannia* it looked as though the 1936 season in England would be an anticlimax after the success of the previous year. It certainly started modestly with only three starters in the Big Class at Harwich – *Endeavour*, *Velsheda*, and *Astra*; and it was the baby of the class, *Astra*, which won the first two races. The reduced fleet then moved down to Southend, and then competed in the historic Nore to Dover race which had not been held for many years. *Velsheda* did well but *Endeavour* was moving so badly it was thought she might have a fouled bottom.

On 24 June *Endeavour II* took part in the West Country regattas at Falmouth and Fowey, but again *Astra* outsailed the fleet during the first race at Falmouth, and was only beaten by the new J in the second and in the one held off Fowey. Now in her ninth season, *Astra* was probably sailing better than in her first. Without a doubt the handicap rating given her under the rule governing 'old' yachts racing with the Js worked strongly in her favour. For instance the fullness in her bows which was so helpful to her in smooth waters as it increased her length should have been penalised under the Universal Rule, but this, under the British variations on the rule, was permitted without penalty. Her time allowance over the Js in 1936 was 8.8 seconds per mile, which amounted to 4 minutes 24 seconds over a 30-mile

135

course – quite sufficient to give her the edge in light weather. The fleet then moved on to Plymouth and it was here that disaster struck, enforcing the growing opinion that the Js were seaworthy in only the fairest of winds: both *Endeavour II* and *Velsheda* were dismasted.

The weather for the regatta had been sufficiently bad for the committee to cancel the first day's racing. It was equally bad the next day, the wind and tide kicking up the steepest sea the Js had ever had to face. According to John Nicholson, Tom Thorneycroft, who was sailing as guest helmsman on *Endeavour*, persuaded the other Js to race. As Nicholson sensibly commented they should have agreed to race with reefed mainsails. Instead *Endeavour II* went out with a whole sail. This, of course, could have been a deliberate test of the rigging. Whatever the reason, the rigging was found wanting because either a fitting on the inner end of the lower cross trees broke off or there was a failure in the cross tree guys. *Endeavour*'s mast pitched over the side. *Velsheda*'s went too but the reason for it doing so was never firmly established.

The outcry in the yachting and daily press was immediate and vehement, and someone coined an unkind couplet that ran:
'When the winds of July and August blow

The masts of most of the J-Class go.'

In fact so much abuse was published about the rigging of the Js that Charles Nicholson, usually a man of few words, felt obliged to enter the arena and clear up some misconceptions. In a sharply-worded letter to a British yachting magazine, in which he pointed out some of the major failures that had occurred to Big Boats in the 1920s, Nicholson stated categorically that the fault did not lie with the masts but 'through failure of some detail of the rigging outfit under exceptional conditions, which disposes of the outcry against the height of masts and of jib-headed mainsails.' He did concede, however, that the high foretriangle allowed under the revised rules after the 1930 challenge – $82\frac{1}{2}\%$ of the height of the mast – had produced stress problems because of the much increased power of the headsails, a point he had raised at the time when he had suggested a maximum height of 75% for the foretriangle.

In many ways it was an unfortunately phrased letter for it was immediately seen that the great designer was splitting hairs. As many people subsequently pointed out, in the matter of safety and seaworthiness a yacht's mast cannot really be considered as being separate from the rigging which supports it. Exaggerated as many of the reports obviously were, and founded in many cases on complete ignorance of the subject, it was now felt by nearly everyone that something had to be done. There were lone voices which said that it was nothing to do with the rig, that if the owners used a degree of seamanship and common sense by reefing there would be no dismastings, but these were in a minority. The general consensus was for change, and, spurred on by the controversy the YRA, held a conference during the 1936 Cowes Week and then came out with a statement that they were investigating the possibility of introducing the L-Class, which had a maximum length of 56 feet.

Two months later a writer in the American magazine *Rudder* commented tartly: 'If anybody has published a kind word for the J-Boats anywhere in the yachting press of either country during the past season, it has escaped my notice . . . from the way masts have been going by the board it is plain they are over-rigged. Perhaps it might be possible to get Mr Henry Ford, the master of mass production, to establish a factory for turning out steel J masts.'

Whatever the result of this controversy, the cause of it – *Endeavour II* and *Velsheda* – were both sailing again in next to no time, Stephenson with a borrowed mast from

Above: Tom Thorneycroft steering *Endeavour*. Seated are the yacht's new owners, Mr and Mrs Herman Andreae. | *Stephenson*

Top left: Endeavour II being taken in tow by Lord Runciman's yacht after being dismasted during the Plymouth Regatta./*Stephenson*

Top centre: Jilling around before the start. From left to right: *Astra, Endeavour* and *Endeavour II. Velsheda* is in the background./*Stephenson*

Bottom left: Herman Andreae at the wheel of *Endeavour*. He laid up *Candida* at the end of 1935 and bought *Endeavour* from T.O.M. Sopwith. Astern is *Velsheda*./*Stephenson*

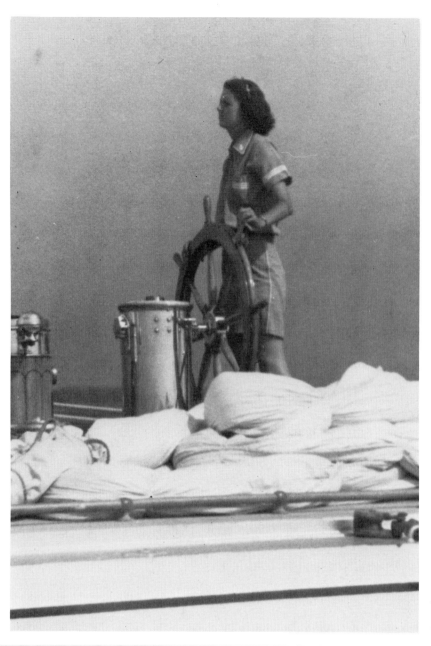

Candida – now laid up and awaiting a buyer – and at Yarmouth *Endeavour* beat *Endeavour II*, with *Astra* third.

Early in the New Year Lambert had reversed his decision to race in British waters in 1936. There were several reasons for this but obviously the Americans wanted him back over on their side if there were to be another challenge, and also Lambert came to the conclusion that it was not proper to remain lest he should be thought to be spying on the potential challenger. So, in April of that year, *Yankee* had returned to Boston.

The lure of racing for the honour to defend the Cup brought out *Weetamoe* and *Rainbow*, which Vanderbilt had bought from the syndicate which had built her in 1934, though neither had been commissioned in 1935 when *Yankee* had been in England. *Yankee* and *Rainbow*, the two most likely candidates for defending the Cup, were asked by the Race Committee of the NYYC to stick together as much as possible in order to ascertain their comparative speeds. This they did and had a very close season's racing winning eight races each, *Rainbow* being the better boat in light airs while *Yankee* maintained her reputation of being the best J on the American side in fresher winds. Both yachts, according to Vanderbilt, were in better shape than they had been in 1934, each having new small-diameter metal masts. In addition *Rainbow* had a ten ton lead shoe fitted under her keel. *Weetamoe* now owned by Chandler Hovey remained unchanged.

While the American Js were enjoying excellent racing in superb conditions the British Js, plus *Astra* were sailing in some of the worst weather for years. But during it *Endeavour II* was proving her superiority over the other two Js for out of ten starts she had won six first flags, and two seconds, against

Velsheda's four wins and a second and *Endeavour*'s one win and nine seconds, both *Velsheda* and *Endeavour* having made sixteen starts.

Then early on in Cowes Week *Endeavour II* lost her mast again. This time the cause was the failure of a backstay winch pawl track, and this cast further gloom on a Cowes Week which was missing its former patron, the Sailor King, and which was further bedevilled by bad weather. As one yachting correspondent put it, a 'vast and unexpected change has come over the maritime sport of Great Britain'.

Endeavour II's dismasting did not prevent Sopwith from issuing his challenge for the following year, and requesting that the races take place in July instead of the traditional month, September. His reasoning was that he hoped to find more wind off Newport in July, and that by arranging to have the challenger in American waters at the beginning of the 1937 season he would have the same amount of time for tuning up as the American defender. The challenge was accepted and so, less willingly, was the date of 31st July for the first race.

The question then arose as to whether any one of the American Js already afloat could successfully defend against the new challenger which, although losing much valuable time through being twice dismasted, was apparently faster than *Endeavour* which had conclusively held *Yankee* the previous season and which had so nearly beaten *Rainbow* in 1934. It was decided that there was not. When it came to the question as to who was then to build a new defender, however, there was hardly a rush to pick up the tab. The worst of the recession might be over but the era of the big spenders was over too. Vanderbilt proposed that if the NYYC could raise half the sum involved – around $200,000 – then he and his family would provide the rest, plus any gear from *Rainbow* that might be of use. It seemed a fair offer but the Js in America were no more popular than they were in England, and no one came forward. In the end Vanderbilt shouldered the whole burden himself.

Back in England the season ended with some fine weather and with the old *Endeavour* at the top of the class, but with the new one the undoubted champion. No one suspected it then but the British public had seen the last of the Big Boats racing in the regatta circuit. Early in 1937 Sopwith left with both *Endeavours* to cross the Atlantic and neither *Velsheda* nor *Shamrock* were fitted out, leaving only *Astra* in commission for Hugh Paul to live on while he raced his new 12-Metre, *Little Astra*. The following year was devoid of Big Boats too, despite Sopwith's invitation to the owners of all the American Js to join him in the regatta circuit in 1938.

There were two important changes to the conditions covering the 1937 challenge. The first one read that 'the challenger shall have the right to substitute another yacht for the yacht named in the challenge (*Endeavour II*) provided notice of this intention is received not less than 30 days before the date of the first race.' The other change was one obviously brought in by the hue and cry raised by the multiplicity of dismastings during the previous season. It involved the weight of the mast of the competing Js. The minimum weight regardless of the size of the boat was abolished and the weight of the mast, including permanent fittings now – not just the bare stick – was made dependent on waterline length. As both challenger and defender were built to the maximum length allowed it meant their masts had to weigh at least 6,400lbs. There were also new restrictions on minimum diameters, and the centre of gravity of the mast was lowered.

Knowing that time was short, Vanderbilt asked Starling Burgess and Olin Stephens, of the firm Sparkman and Stephens, to start on the design of a new defender while the NYYC were still trying to form a syndicate. He said he would pay any out-of-pocket expenses but that the execution of the design and construction contracts had to wait until the syndicate was formed. Both designers agreed to this plan.

Vanderbilt had decided on the team of Burgess and Stephens because he wanted a younger man to have some experience in designing a J-boat. Stephens was the obvious choice. Not only was he the top young designer of his day he was also closely allied with Professor Davidson in carrying out tank tests at the Stevens Institute. Although the model chosen was Burgess's it is generally agreed that Stephen's youthful genius and influence on the older designer produced a more revolutionary design than if Burgess had been working on his own.

It was agreed that each designer would draw four sets of lines and that models would then be made from these for towing tests in the tank at the Stevens Institute. Clinton Crane lent his model of *Weetamoe* to Stephens, and Burgess and Nicholson had exchanged the lines of their respective craft after the 1934 challenge, so it was decided to build models of *Endeavour* and *Rainbow* and test all seven models for comparison. Both Stephens and Burgess were given complete freedom in designing their two sets of lines each, the only restrictions being that the designs would be 87ft on the waterline, that they would have a deep forefoot and a moderate beam. The deep forefoot was to increase stability, a point on

Top left: There was not as much competition for Vanderbilt in 1937 as there had been in 1930 and 1934, but this didn't mean the other American Js were lying idle. Here Sis Hovey is at *Rainbow*'s helm during a friendly duel. Probably Sis Hovey and Mrs Sopwith were the only women who raced Js regularly. In 1937 Chandler Hovey owned both *Weetamoe* and *Rainbow./Morss*

Bottom left: Endeavour II was dismasted twice during the 1936 season. The second time was during the Royal London Yacht Club Regatta at Cowes. / *The Times*

Drawn by our Special Artist, G. H. Davis.

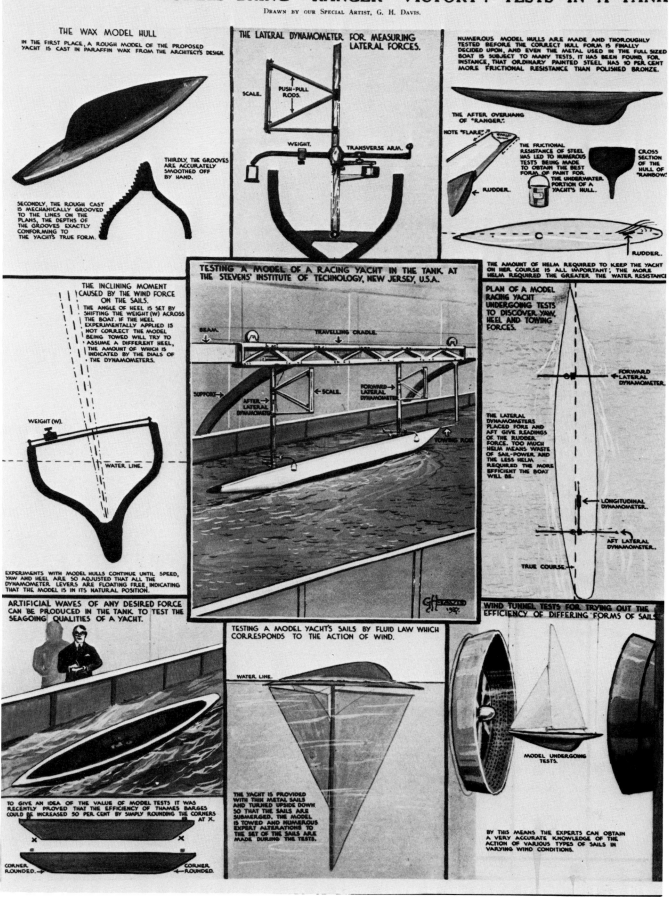

which Vanderbilt admitted being a 'crank', as he put it, after adding five tons of ballast to *Rainbow* the day before the Astor Cup Race in 1934 and winning it and many subsequent races.

Initially there was some concern that an 87ft waterline boat would behave creditably in light airs but after Vanderbilt had experimented with *Rainbow* in 1936 by ballasting her down to 87 feet and finding her light weather performance remarkably good, everyone felt more certain the choice had been the correct one. By encouraging a moderate beam in the designs Vanderbilt hoped to eliminate *Yankee*'s trait of not performing at her best in light airs.

The year 1937 was the first in which scientific tank testing was carried out allowing for all the factors involved. Tests, of course, had been carried out for many years, but large models of between ten and twenty feet had had to be used and were expensive. Further, because all the factors causing resistance had not been taken into account, they had not proved accurate. But during the thirties Professor Davidson had managed to develop much smaller – three foot – models, which, so Clinton Crane reckoned, only cost $50 against many thousands. More important, Davidson invented a method whereby the lateral force of the wind on a hull could be applied to a model as well as the normal forward thrust resulting from it at differing degrees of heel. His experiments, which included this new factor, showed that the lateral thrust increased the resistance on the hull but not in a way that could be measured by getting the results of towing a model in the normal manner. When the models of *Rainbow, Endeavour* and *Weetamoe* were tested by these new methods it was found that on the wind *Endeavour* was slightly superior to *Rainbow* at all speeds and that *Rainbow* was slightly superior to *Weetamoe*. This encouraged Vanderbilt and his design team as these results corresponded with their observations of these three Js in actual racing conditions. They felt they could commit the new designs to the testing tank in the knowledge that it would produce reliable results.

Of the four models tested, one, the Burgess design 77-C, showed a marked superiority at speeds between six and eight knots, though more resistance at over eleven knots than one of the other designs. 77-C was selected and the designers then tried to improve on this model but were unable to do so. Some say they sought not so much to improve it but to erase some of the model's remarkably ugly features. But it was subsequently thought that it was her bulbous stem and flattened stern that were in fact responsible for her remarkable speed on the wind.

Olin Stephens confirms that model 77-C was one of Burgess's. But though both designers were responsible for producing their own models there was a constant interplay of ideas and Stephens comments that he probably influenced the lower stern afterbody profile of the model as he had been using similar lines in his 6-Metre designs and had incorporated this feature in his models for the new J.

'The model selected,' Burgess commented, 'was so unusual that I do not think any one of us would have dared to pick her had we not had the tank results and Kenneth Davidson's analysis to back her,' and Stephens commented that he found the accuracy of the tests 'really amazing', though adding that 'the tanks will not design a boat; it will answer a question,' and that that question had to be carefully framed.

By the autumn the lines for *Ranger* had been decided but not, unfortunately, who would pay for her design and construction. It looked at one point as if there would not be a new defender. But then the President of the Bath Iron Works in Maine – where it had been proposed *Ranger* would be built – stepped in and said he would build the new J on a cost-only basis. This, plus the designers' offer to reduce their fees, influenced Vanderbilt sufficiently for him to agree to pick up the tab for the whole Cup defence – which must have amounted to nearly half a million dollars.

Ranger, unlike previous defenders, was of all-steel construction with flush-riveted plating, and Vanderbilt remarked on the tremendous care the builders had taken in making her as fair and as smooth as possible. Her spars, including the main boom and spinnaker booms, were made of duralumin. Her bar rigging and many of her other fittings came from *Rainbow*. Many of her sails, too, came from Vanderbilt's earlier Js, *Enterprise* and *Rainbow* – indeed not one of her four mainsails was new – but as the season progressed Vanderbilt was forced to replace most of them because he found *Ranger* could take and needed more powerful headsails than his earlier boats could use.

Ranger was launched on 11th May, and a few days later, her mast in place, she was taken in tow for the voyage round Cape Cod to Newport. *Vara*, which was towing *Ranger*, ran into an unpleasant sea and fog, and when Rod Stephens, who was in charge of the operation, heard in the dark the tinkling of loose metal, he knew *Ranger* was in trouble. An emergency flare was eventually lit on the J, and *Vara* stopped and played her searchlight onto her. Stephens could then see that some of the upper parts of the rod rigging had worked loose and had come undone so that the top seventy feet of the mast on the

Left: How tank testing worked. Drawn by an *Illustrated London News* artist. /*Illustrated London News*

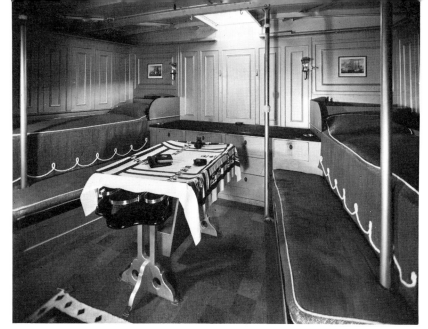

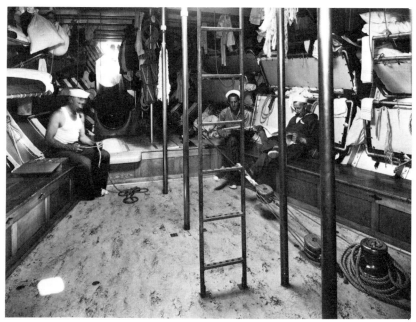

port side no longer had any support. He immediately ordered *Vara* to head for the nearest port, but in the swell and the wind more rigging came adrift, and at 0645 with 'a report like a cannon' the mast snapped about thirty-five feet above the deck and pitched over the side. The crew were forced to cut it loose and it went to the bottom.

The first informal races were due to take place less than two weeks later so the accident was a disaster for Vanderbilt. New plates were ordered and the Bath Works were alerted to make a new mast and rigging, and this they managed to do in the remarkably short time of twenty-five days.

In the meantime Vanderbilt decided to step *Rainbow*'s 1934 duralumin mast which had not been sold to *Rainbow*'s new owner, Chandler Hovey, as *Rainbow* now had her new circular steel mast. But at this point the other two J-boat owners showed their sportsmanship by offering to lend whatever gear they were not themselves using and agreeing between themselves to delay the preliminary races by four days and the Observation Races by a week. So when *Ranger*'s temporary mast was stepped it was rigged with standing rigging from *Enterprise, Vanitie* and *Weetamoe*. Nevertheless, she won all four preliminary races against the other two Js, and proved to her owner and the Race Committee that she was a remarkably fast boat, superior to the other Js in every point of sailing in any strength of breeze – with the exception of *Yankee* which held her own when running.

Between the preliminary races and the observation races, *Ranger* stepped her new mast and bar rigging. Subsequently she won all the observation races with even greater

Top: Ranger's accommodation was luxurious. This is the owner's stateroom./*Rosenfeld*

Above: The crew's quarters were comfortable too. Note the sail chute./*Rosenfeld*

Right: Launching *Ranger* on 11th May 1937. The wedges lifted the keel off the ground just enough for the yacht to be launched./*Arthur Knapp Jr.*

142

Above: After *Ranger*'s launching, left to right: Olin Stephens, Rod Stephens, Harold S. Vanderbilt, Starling Burgess./*Arthur Knapp Jr.*

ease than she had the earlier series. The only problem she had was keeping her bottom clean, for unlike the bronze of the previous defenders, which was simply polished, *Ranger*'s bottom had to be painted. It did not prove satisfactory, and *Ranger* had to be hauled out and scrubbed, and repainted every two weeks.

But in every other way the new J was ideal. 'After sailing *Ranger* for a couple of days,' Vanderbilt wrote, 'I became convinced that she was totally different from any J-boat I had ever handled. Over a period of years, I had not noticed any very marked difference between *Enterprise*, *Weetamoe* (which he helmed frequently between 1931 and 1933) and *Rainbow*. They all responded in much the same way and felt about the same. But *Ranger* was totally different.' She was, he said, slower to turn and to pick up speed, but held her way longer, and she was perfectly balanced on the wind so long as she was kept going.

But one peculiarity he noticed in particular: when moving fast on any point of sailing she would 'squat down and go', using nearly all of her overall length. Vanderbilt could not account for this trait.

The Official Trials began on 3rd July and were due to continue until the Cup Committee selected the defender. In the first race *Ranger* – racing *Yankee* – beat the previous America's Cup course record which *Yankee* had held since 1930 by 4 minutes 16 seconds, after averaging 11.01 knots on the 20-mile course. Though the wind on this occasion was only 12.5mph at the start and 19mph at the finish.

In 1930 it had been blowing at a steady 28mph, which shows how remarkably fast the later Js were. On 5th July *Ranger* raced *Rainbow* and was beating her on all points of sailing when the time limit expired. Another race was arranged but this was cancelled through lack of wind. The Committee felt, however, they had in any case seen enough

Above: Ranger slicing through the water. She was almost the perfect J./*Rosenfeld*

Top right: The start of a Nichols Cup Race: *Ranger, Rainbow* and – nearest the committee boat – *Yankee*. *Ranger*'s way is greater than the others because she was towed at full speed by *Bystander*, her tender, up to just a few seconds before the five minute gun. This was perfectly legal – it still is – and typical of Vanderbilt's astute racing tactics./*Arthur Knapp Jr.*

Bottom right: The famous victory photograph taken on board *Ranger*. From left to right: Rod Stephens, Olin Stephens, Zenas Bliss, Mrs Vanderbilt, Harold S. Vanderbilt, and Arthur Knapp./*Rosenfeld*

and they nominated *Ranger* as the defender on 6th July. This time no one complained about the hurried selection. *Ranger* had, as Vanderbilt put it, 'selected herself', and once more his afterguard was the top team available; Olin and Rod Stephens, Arthur Knapp as relief helmsman; Zenas Bliss as navigator again; and Vanderbilt himself, and his wife.

There was little doubt in anyone's mind that *Ranger* was the superior boat but Vanderbilt's job was made easier in 1937 than it had been in either 1930 or 1934 because the opposition was much weaker. *Rainbow* had greatly improved since 1934 but no amount of alteration could make her into a real winner, while *Weetamoe* was now on the old side and was not large enough to carry the powerful new sails that had been developed. This left *Yankee*, the yacht which had nearly snatched the honour of defending the Cup from under Vanderbilt's nose in 1934, and had proved herself the equal of *Endeavour* in the British boat's home waters. When Vanderbilt heard that she had again been extensively altered for the 1937 trials, and was allegedly tacking in six and a half points, he told Lambert much later that he had been scared to death! But he had no cause to be.

Yankee was ballasted down almost to the maximum waterline length of 87 feet, and the loose ballast inside her was removed and a lead pad attached to the bottom of her keel instead. This lowered the centre of gravity and stiffened her so that she could carry the new sail plan Lambert had had designed for

her. The mast was then moved forward six feet, and ten feet was added to the boom increasing the area of the mainsail by 500sq ft. The forestay was removed and the mast reinforced to compensate for it. The idea behind all this was to be able to race with a single-headed rig, thus obtaining greater ease of handling and extra driving power from the larger mainsail. A new two-speed winch was installed to cope with the huge new headsails, mainly genoa jibs. It was a powerful device with three handles that involved twelve men in its handling; in its lower gear it had nearly enough power to pull the mast down! But all these enormously expensive alterations failed, and Lambert was soon forced to revert to his previous rig. It is interesting that it was *Ranger* which evolved towards the modern sail plan of large headsails and comparatively small mainsails, while her chief rival went the wrong way, or partly the wrong way, by trying to increase the size and power of her main as well.

In the three weeks remaining before the Cup races began, Vanderbilt went on the Eastern Yacht Club Cruise in order to tune up his creation. She raced against the two *Endeavours* as well as the other American Js and it was during this cruise that she suffered the first of her two defeats of the whole season at the hands of *Endeavour*.

The fleet that set out from England in 1937 to challenge for the Cup was a considerable one. Sopwith had chosen not to tune up *Endeavour II* in England but to take her across

the Atlantic at the beginning of the season and tune her up on the American side. In order to do this properly he got his business partner, Fred Sigrist, to charter *Endeavour* from her new owner Hermann Andreae for the nominal sum of £1, so that *Endeavour II* would have a trial horse in America. Indeed, when both yachts started off across the Atlantic, it was not known which would be the challenger. *Endeavour* was towed by *Viva*, Sopwith's old diesel yacht but now owned by Sigrist, and *Endeavour II* was towed by a deep sea trawler. Hugh Paul lent his skipper from *Astra*, Ted Heard, who skippered *Endeavour*, while *Endeavour II* was skippered by Captain Williams. Altogether there were more than one hundred men.

Both yachts arrived in America at the end of May, *Endeavour II* arriving first as the old challenger was forced to slip her tow in heavy weather and made most of the voyage under her own sail. Both yachts on arrival were hauled out and made ready at Herreshoff's yard at Bristol, Mass. The spirits of the large British contingent were high. Never before had a Cup challenge been so scrupulously prepared, nor for so long. No detail had been overlooked in the effort to give the new challenger every possible aid. *Endeavour II* and her trial horse were even linked by radio. In fact by the date of the first race for the Cup there was no doubt in anybody's mind that the whichever boat was chosen to be the official challenger she

would be perfectly tuned. And indeed this was the case.

The trouble this time lay not in the construction of the boat, the crew, or the temperament of the owner, but in her design. It was acknowledged afterwards that there was nothing to choose between the two crews and, though *Endeavour*'s afterguard (consisting of Sir Ralph Gore as relief helmsman, Frank Murdoch, Wing Commander Scarlett as navigator, and for the last two races, Charles Nicholson) were still less democratically organised than *Ranger*'s team of experts, they were nevertheless very efficient at their jobs. It was just that their boat compared with *Ranger* was as out-of-date as a dinosaur. In four straight races she was beaten by 17 minutes five seconds, 18 minutes 32 seconds, 4 minutes 27 seconds, and 3 minutes 37 seconds.

Yet over the decades Nicholson had produced some superb designs for all types of boat, and in *Endeavour* he had delivered to Sopwith a J that could have, should have, brought back the Cup. But the fact is that *Ranger* was a product of a country that was moving into the new scientific era while *Endeavour II* was the product of a country still thinking of yacht design as an art. So when Nicholson first saw *Ranger* out of the water and said that she was 'the biggest advance in yacht design for fifty years', it sounds as if he was still judging yacht design by artistic progression instead of by the quantum leap

which modern science had given it. It probably would have taken fifty years by normal empirical methods to have progressed to a design like *Ranger*, but with tank-testing Stephens and Burgess had used science – not their artistic intuition – as their guide to choosing the defender's lines.

But not only was *Ranger*'s hull form superior to her challenger's, her sails were better too, for she had more of them and they were more powerful than the British boat's. *Ranger*'s staysail was much larger than her rival's and it was estimated that at times the American was setting as much as one thousand square feet more sail on her foretriangle than the challenger. Yachting correspondents noted that *Endeavour II* had 'plenty of holes' in her foretriangle sailplan 'caused by high-cut "quads" and small staysails.' *Ranger* also had in her sail locker a rayon quad-genoa* and the world's largest spinnaker of 18,000sq ft and her smallest quadrilateral was as big as *Rainbow*'s largest. *Ranger*'s ballooners and parachute spinnakers were superior to the British boat's too, though on one, just one, occasion, with a ballooner set, *Endeavour II* on one ten mile stretch of the course clipped half a minute off the American boat's time. As the Royal Yacht Squadron's

*This was a large overlapping quadrilateral jib which had a greater sail area aloft than was normal. It was first developed by Lambert for *Yankee*.

Top left: Endeavour II about to set off back across the Atlantic. It was a voyage that ended in tragedy./*Murdoch*

Centre left: Endeavour II picking up her tow for the Atlantic crossing./*Murdoch*

Bottom left: Endeavour II broke her Park Avenue boom during her tune up in American waters. Here it is at the Herreshoff yard, June 1937./*Hammond*

Below: On board Endeavour II just two weeks before the first race for the America's Cup. From left to right: Captain Williams, Sir Ralph Gore, Frank Murdoch and, at the helm, T.O.M. Sopwith./*The Times*

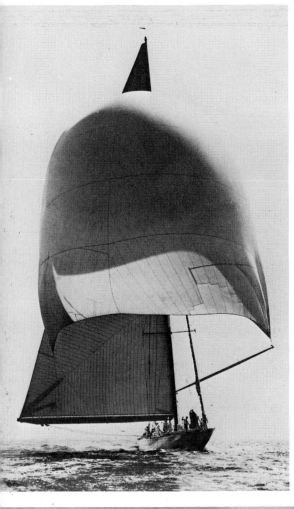

Above left: Ranger's huge
18,000 sq.ft. spinnaker./*Beken*

Above: Endeavour II had a
spinnaker the same size but it
was not as effective./*Murdoch*

Left: Vara towing *Ranger* to
starting line for the third
America's Cup Race. Training
was so intense that the
afterguard, who lived on board
Vara, during one stint never
stepped ashore for two weeks.
The crew lived aboard
Ranger./Arthur Knapp Jr.

Far left: Endeavour II with her
18,000 sq. ft. spinnaker. The
foot measured 150 feet./
Murdoch

representative on board *Ranger*, Sir Fisher Dilke, said, the ballooner should have gone into a museum for that reason alone.

Interest in the Cup races that year was intense amongst the American public for everyone must have thought that at last Britain really had a chance of taking the Cup back across the Atlantic. Thousands of water-borne spectators flocked to see the start of the first race. It was an exotic sight and as one yachting correspondent noted 'where else would you find two full-rigged ships, the *Joseph Conrad* and the *Seven Seas*, keeping company with a houseboat which had put to sea with a car parked in its garage on the afterdeck?'

The crowds however quickly drifted away when it was obvious that the Cup was going to stay where it was, and by 5th August the races were over.

On 16th August both British Js as well as the American boats, *Yankee*, *Rainbow*, and *Ranger* took part in the New York Yacht Club Cruise in which *Ranger* won every race except the New London to Newport which *Yankee* won. *Endeavour II*, showing she was at least the second fastest J-boat afloat, came second seven times out of eleven starts, the other second places being taken by *Rainbow* twice and *Yankee* and *Ranger* once each. As Vanderbilt remarked, the other Js got so used to *Ranger* winning that the real battle was for second place. *Ranger* raced thirty-seven times in all that season, and she was only beaten twice. A remarkable record.

Altogether the failure of the challenge was a disaster for the British contingent, and added to a humiliating defeat was the tragedy of the loss of two of their crew members.

Above: *Ranger* finishing eighteen minutes ahead of the challenger in the second race. A small foresail has been set inside her huge silk quadrilateral./*Illustrated London News*

Right: New York Yacht Club Cruise in Buzzards Bay. *Rainbow* is to windward, then comes *Endeavour*, *Ranger*, *Endeavour II*, and *Yankee*./*Arthur Knapp Jr.*

Above: One of the starts during the New York Yacht Club cruise. Furthest from the camera is *Rainbow*. Next is *Endeavour*, then *Ranger*, *Endeavour II*, and *Yankee*. When Vanderbilt sold *Rainbow* to Chandler Hovey he retained the number 5 for *Ranger*./*Rosenfeld*

Left: New York Yacht Club cruise in Buzzards Bay. *Ranger* leading on first leeward leg, followed by *Rainbow*, *Endeavour II* and *Yankee*. Note the bowsprit on *Ranger*. This was a very light temporary pole to prevent the spinnaker from being drawn under the bows if it collapsed. It never did! / *Arthur Knapp Jr.*

151

While in America *Endeavour*'s navigator, Captain MacPhee, died from a ruptured ulcer and the same affliction caused the death of Captain Williams on the voyage home when *Endeavour II* and *Philante*, which was towing her, were caught in bad weather. It was a grim time for all concerned with the captain dying below and three men on deck clinging to the wheel and having to be relieved every twenty minutes.

Meanwhile *Endeavour*, under Ted Heard, had been forced to cast off her tow when she and *Vita* were hit by a hurricane coming up from the West Indies. For nine days she was lost from the world and many feared she had foundered. But the J-Class hull proved again to be much stronger than its racing rig, and *Endeavour* eventually reappeared none the worse for her battering to receive a hero's welcome home.

This Certifies That

ARTHUR KNAPP Jr

Was one of the **RANGER BOYS,** crew of the 1937 America's Cup Defender "Ranger," and that his services were first class in every respect.

Geo. H. Monsell   **MASTER.**

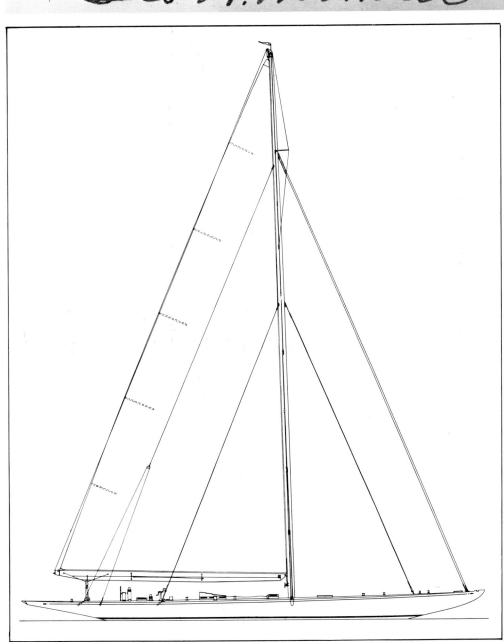

Above: Each member of *Ranger*'s crew and afterguard were given this card by Vanderbilt after the 1937 series./*Arthur Knapp Jr.*

Far left top: A bird's-eye view of the Js in action during the New York Yacht Club Cruise, 1937./*Yachting*

Far left bottom: The America's Cup decided, now was the time to relax: the challenger's afterguard take it easy on the New York Yacht Club cruise. Mrs Sopwith is with her sister, Frank Murdoch and Dr Peter Milligan. *Endeavour II*'s owner is sitting on a winch, and Sir Ralph Gore, The Royal Yacht Squadron's official observer during the series, stands by the binnacle. Captain Williams is at the wheel./*Murdoch*

Left: Ranger's sail plan./*Olin Stephens*

Epilogue–
Whatever became of the Js ?

Much has happened with the surviving J-class yachts since the first edition of this book. Then, it seemed as if only one, *Shamrock*, at that time called *Quadrifoglio*, would ever sail again and that none could ever be put back into racing trim, and I said this. How wrong one can be, and how glad I am that I was.

In 1974 a million pound refit was started on *Quadrifoglio* at her original builders, Camper & Nicholson. However, she was not rerigged as a J-class yacht for she was given a shorter mast, of 153 feet, high bulwarks, two GN V6 200hp engines, and a larger deckhouse, making her an ideal cruising yacht for the Mediterranean where her Italian owner based her after her relaunch in 1980. She is now called by her original name, *Shamrock V*, and has the most up-to-date aids to seamanship including satellite navigational equipment, and her accommodation has been thoroughly modernised, though the silver-plated door furniture and bird's eye maple panelling has been retained in the main saloon. In the spring of 1986 she was purchased by the Museum of Yachting at Newport, Rhode Island, with the help of a grant from the Lipton Tea Company and there is a possibility that she may eventually be refitted as a J-class yacht once more.

Velsheda, too, is now afloat again and has taken part in Tall Ship races. Her present owner, an Englishman, spent several years restoring her himself exactly to her original rig, and she was relaunched in 1983. She may not have the lavish fittings of *Shamrock V* but she is a genuine J-class yacht still, and is a wonderful sight on the water.

But perhaps the most dramatic transformation of all is that of *Endeavour*. After passing through several hands postwar, steadily deteriorating all the time, she was eventually bought by an Englishman whose dream it was to restore her to her original condition and to have her classified '100 A1' at Lloyds. Sadly, his funds ran out, but happily his work was not wasted for the partially restored *Endeavour* was bought by an American yachtswoman who has had the money and the dedication to fulfil the yacht's previous owner's dream. *Endeavour* was relaunched in August 1986 and is to be lavishly refitted below on the Continent. Her accommodation will include a master suite and four guest staterooms, a marble-faced fireplace in the saloon, and a dining table which seats ten. Forward of the mast will be crew accommodation for ten, a far smaller number

than originally, but then they will have hydraulically driven winches and the most modern coffee grinders to help them. Her original J-class rig will be restored – including a 175-foot mast of extruded aluminium, a 51-foot spinnaker pole and a Park Avenue boom. What will not be original is the Caterpillar 3406 turbo-charged 400hp diesel engine that will be installed in her, but this will not stop her racing. In fact, her owner has been the instigator in forming the J-class Society consisting of other J-class owners who, it is planned, will compete against each other during some of the world's most famous regattas. It is an exciting thought.

If the plans of the Society come to fruition, *Endeavour* will possibly have *Astra* to compete against as well as *Shamrock V* and *Velsheda*, for her new Italian owner is considering refitting her with her original racing rig. Perhaps *Candida*, too, would be able to join in for though she is now a yawl-rigged cruiser she is still in excellent condition and could probably be restored to her original racing rig without vast expenditure. Finally, plans are afoot to restore *Lulworth*, after being used for many years as a houseboat. Although she was never converted to the J-class she would be a splendid addition to the growing band of renovated Big Class yachts from the inter-war years.

Of the other great yachts described in this book sadly very little remains. *Cambria* is still around, but *Endeavour II*, after languishing for years as a houseboat in the south coast mud, was scrapped in 1968, while in America not one J boat remains. *Whirlwind* and *Enterprise* were scrapped in 1935 at City Island and Bristol respectively; *Weetamoe* went the same way in 1938, and then *Vanitie* and *Resolute* in 1939, *Rainbow* in 1940, and, finally, *Ranger* and *Yankee* in 1941.

In a letter Captain George Monsell wrote to a friend he said that Lambert's 'lovely gesture this week was splendid – *Atlantic* and *Utilitie* to the US Coast Guard, *Yankee* to the knackers and the money to build a spitfire for knocking over one fritz or two.' But in his autobiography Lambert says he gave the money he received from scrapping *Yankee* to 'Queen Mary of England, to be used at her discretion in the London Hospital. I happened to know that this hospital was her favourite activity. I sent it to her as money coming from the yacht *Yankee* in memory of the courtesies shown *Yankee* by King George and herself.'

Opposite, top left: Endeavour being renovated at Calshot. This photograph was taken in 1983 while she was still in British ownership. Nearly all her original frames and plating have had to be replaced./author

Opposite, top right: Norlanda. ex-Candida, in the Mediterranean where she is based. She is in excellent condition./Camper & Nicholson, Cannes

Opposite, bottom: Endeavour being relaunched from Calshot August 1986. Her American owner plans to have her sailing – and racing – in 1988./KOS Photos

155

Above: Quadrifoglio, ex-Shamrock, ex-Shamrock V, coming alongside at Southampton after her voyage from Italy in 1974. It took six years to restore her./Quilter

Centre right: Endeavour before restoration began./Beken

Below right: Weetamoe being dismantled, 3rd May 1938. / Yachting

Opposite, top: Endeavour II being broken up at Southampton, 1968./Tudor House Museum, Southampton, and George Cohen & Co. Ltd.

Opposite, bottom: Astra in the Mediterranean during the 1970s. She is now being restored to her original rig by her new Italian owner./Countess Matarazzo

Acknowledgements

I would like to thank here all those people on both sides of the Atlantic who helped me piece together the story of the J-Class. It is just not possible to name everyone but I am especially grateful to my wife, Wendy, for expert editing; to Gerald Pollinger who prompted me to start; to Frank Murdoch for being so generous with his time and advice and for reading the manuscript; to 'Skipper' Stroud for allowing me to quote from his manuscript; to Christopher Boardman, Arthur Knapp Jnr., and many others for so kindly lending me their photographs for reproduction in this book; to Olin Stephens for reading the manuscript and writing the foreword; to Sir Thomas Sopwith and the surviving members of the afterguard and crews of the J-Class both here and in the United States for their anecdotes and memories; to the secretaries of the Cruising Association in London and the New York Yacht Club in New York, and to Mr Ruvigny of *The Field*, for allowing me the use of their libraries; and finally to all the people on both sides of the Atlantic who answered my plea in the correspondence columns of the yachting magazines for information on the J-Class. Without the help of all these people this book would never have been written.

Ian Dear
London, November 1976

Opposite, top: Until bought for renovation in the early 1980s, *Velsheda* lay for many years in a mud berth on the Hamble./ *Eastland*

Opposite, bottom left: The renovated *Shamrock V* in the Solent, 1980. Like *Endeavour*, she is now American owned./ *Beken*

Opposite, bottom right: *Velsheda*, now restored to her original racing rig, under way in the Solent in 1985./*KOS Photos*

Bibliography

Atkins, J. B. *Further Memorials of the Royal Yacht Squadron*. Geoffrey Bles, London. 1939.

Brooks, Jerome. *The $30,000,000 Cup*. Simon & Schuster, New York. 1958.

Crane, Clinton. *Yachting Memories*. Van Nostrand, New York. 1952.

Dilke, Sir Fisher. *Observer on Ranger*. Herbert Jenkins, London. 1938.

Dixon, Douglas. *The King's Sailing Master*. Harrap, London. 1948.

Gliksman, Alain. *Beken of Cowes 1919-1939*. Cassell, London. 1969.

Fox, Uffa. *Sailing, Seamanship & Yacht Construction*. Peter Davies, London. 1934.

Fox, Uffa. *Second Book*. Peter Davies, London. 1935.

Fox, Uffa. *Sail and Power*. Peter Davies, London. 1936.

Fox, Uffa. *Racing, Cruising & Design* Peter Davies, London 1937.

Heckstall-Smith, Anthony. *Sacred Cowes* (rev. ed.). Anthony Blond, London. 1965.

Heckstall-Smith, Brooke. *Britannia and her Contemporaries*. Methuen, London. 1927.

Herreshoff, L. Francis. *The Common Sense of Yacht Designs Vols: 1 & 2*. Rudder, New York. 1948.

Hoyt, Sherman. *Memoirs*. Published in U.K. as *Yankee Yachtsman* by Robert Cross, London in 1951. Van Nostrand, New York. 1950.

Irving, John. *The King's Britannia*. Seeley, Service, London. 1936.

Lambert, Gerard. *All out of Step*. Doubleday, New York. 1958.

Lambert, Gerard. *Yankee in England*. Doubleday, New York. 1937.

Nicholson, John. *Great Years in Yachting*. Nautical Publishing Co. 1970.

Parkinson, John J. *History of the New York Yacht Club*. New York Yacht Club. 1974.

Scott Hughes, John. *Come and Sail*. Museum Press, London. 1953.

Scott Hughes, John. *Sailing Through Life*. Methuen, London. 1947.

Vanderbilt, Harold. *Enterprise*. Scribner, New York. 1931.

Vanderbilt, Harold. *On the Wind's Highway*. Scribner, New York. 1939.

Waugh, Alec. *The Lipton Story*. Doubleday, New York. 1950. and Cassell, London, 1951.

Wentworth Day, J. *King George V as a Sportsman*. Cassell, London. 1935.

Yachtsman's Year Book. Dodd, Mead, New York. 1935 and 1936.

Index
of yachts, their designers, builders, owners and crew